CHINA MIRACLE

ARTHUR WALLIS

CHINA

MIRACLE

A Silent Explosion

Cityhill
PUBLISHING

Columbia, Missouri

Cityhill Publishing
4600 Christian Fellowship Road
Columbia, Mo. 65203

Published in Great Britain by
Kingsway Publications Ltd.

ISBN 0-939159-00-7

Unless otherwise indicated, biblical quotations are from
the New International Version, ©New York International
Bible Society 1978.

RSV = Revised Standard Version
copyrighted 1946, 1952, 1971, 1973, by the
Division of Christian Education of the National
Council of the Churches of Christ in the USA

NASB = New American Standard Bible
© The Lockman Foundation 1960, 1962, 1963, 1968,
1971, 1972, 1973

TLB = The Living Bible
© Tyndale House Publishers 1971

NEB = New English Bible
© The Delegates of the Oxford University Press and the Syndics
of the Cambridge University Press 1961, 1970

Front cover: Chinese character means "hope"

THE CHURCH IN CHINA

"Hard pressed on every side, but not crushed; perplexed, but not in despair; persecuted, but not abandoned; struck down, but not destroyed"— across the divide men call the "Bamboo Curtain" you speak to us who dwell in the ease and comfort of the West. With all your deprivations and restrictions, you demonstrate to us something of the rugged grandeur of New Testament Christianity, that we, with all our privileges, so sadly lack—

to you this book is affectionately dedicated.

THANK YOU

To Paul Kauffman, whose book, *China: The Emerging Challenge*, was my early inspiration, and who was such an encouragement to me when we met in Hong Kong.

To others whose books have greatly helped me, especially Leslie Lyall's *God Reigns in China*, David Adeney's *Christian Students Face the Revolution*, and Carl Lawrence's *The Church in China*. Where I have been granted permission to quote from these and other writings, this has been acknowledged in the footnotes.

To various China Ministries in Hong Kong, especially the Chinese Church Research Center, Christian Communications, Asian Outreach, and Open Doors, whose communications have given me up-to-date information about the church on the mainland.

To David Wang for his help and encouragement, and especially for the transcript of a message on what God is saying to us through the church in China.

To Ross Paterson, who generously put his China material at my disposal and put me in touch with Tony Lambert. To them both for reading my script with great care and putting me right on a number of details.

To Alan Boardman for the map of China.

To Diana Moss for all her typing and re-typing.

Last, but by no means least, to my wife and partner in the work, Eileen, who has been a constant source of help and encouragement.

CONTENTS

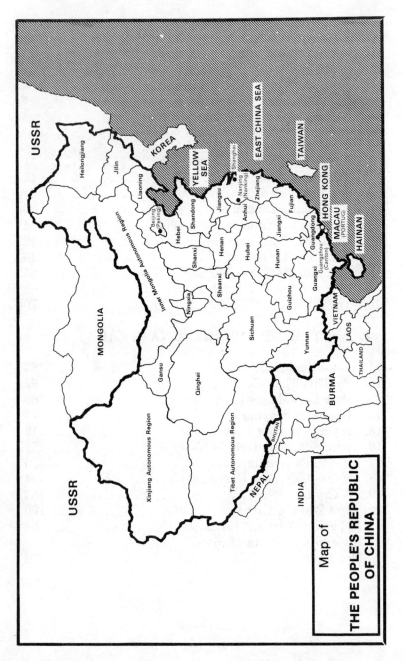

Map of

THE PEOPLE'S REPUBLIC OF CHINA

PART ONE

China Tells Her Story

1

WHY "CHINA MIRACLE"?

*Who among the Gods is like you, O
Lord? Who is like you—majestic in
holiness, awesome in glory, working
wonders?*

Exodus 15:11

Many believers are aware that recently there has been some
kind of revival of Christianity in China. But how extensive
is it? Is there really any justification for describing it as "a
miracle"? Let us answer that by considering for a moment
the circumstances in which God has been working.

On my first visit to China I was agreeably surprised at
the freedom there appeared to be. It seemed I could go
anywhere and speak to anyone without restriction. "I've
never been to Russia," I remarked to a leading correspondent
in Beijing (Peking), "but I would imagine there is much more
freedom here in China." He shook his head and smiled.
"You don't understand how the system works. It is not you
they are watching so much as the Chinese people who talk to
you. They could well be required, after you have gone, to
explain their contact with a foreigner."

I soon discovered that there was a nationwide spy
system. As a Chinese citizen, any suspicious action where
you live could be reported to your street committee. Any
irregularities at your workplace could be reported to your
"danwei," or work committee. There they would have a
complete dossier on you. In effect, everybody spies on
everybody else. You are not free to get engaged, marry,
move, change jobs, and so on, without reference to your

danwei. The People's Republic is changing, but it has been
one of the most repressive and restrictive regimes in the
world. It is in this political context that God has been at
work.

On top of all that, the darkest period of the church in China
during the thirty-five years of Communist rule was the
"Great Cultural Revolution." Churches were compulsorily
closed, pastors imprisoned, and bonfires made of Bibles and
Christian books. It seemed to outside observers that the
church in China had been wiped out. For God to revive His
church in the normal political context of Communist China
would have been remarkable, but the resurrection of His
church from the ashes of the Cultural Revolution must be
regarded as nothing short of a miracle.

Geographically, China is one of the largest countries in
the world. The movement of the Holy Spirit has not been
confined to a few bright spots, nor even to the areas where
missionaries formerly labored. It has reached almost all of
China's twenty-nine provinces, autonomous regions, and
municipalities—from the desolate steppes of Inner Mongolia
in the north to the mountain tribes of the southwest; and
from the coastal provinces with their teeming millions to the
mountainous borders of Tibet. The incredible range of this
movement qualifies it to be called a miracle.

Furthermore, China is numerically the greatest nation,
with its "one billion plus" population. One out of every four
human beings is Chinese. When the Communists came to
power in 1949 there were approximately four million
Catholics and one million Protestants in China, but this
figure was drastically reduced during the Cultural
Revolution. By 1983 it was estimated that there were
probably fifty million Bible-believing Christians, or 5% of
the population.

When you consider that this phenomenal multiplication
occurred when so many pastors and mature leaders were in
prison and when Bibles and Christian literature were in
grievously short supply, that must surely be a miracle by
any standards. The movement has been described as "the
most rapid church growth in the history of Christianity."
Others have pointed out that the church in China now

represents the largest body of believers in the world.

As a young Christian I had read most of the great missionary biographies dealing with China—Hudson Taylor, the Cambridge Seven, *The Triumph of John and Betty Stam*, as well as those of the great Chinese leaders, Pastor Hsi, John Sung, and most notably the teachings of Watchman Nee. The "magic and mystique of China" fascinated and frightened me. "It must be a wonderful country," I thought. "But I just hope I'm not called to be a missionary there. Too many never come back!"

Now I was finding the reports coming out of China thrilling. "One day," wrote Brother Andrew, in his magazine *Open Doors*, "perhaps quite soon, someone will write about this revival, and we shall advertise the book." As I read those words, a voice within said, "You do it!" I was taken completely by surprise. Never had I received such a sudden and unexpected commission. Was it really God?

At this point, God and I had a little altercation. Who was I to write such a book? What did I really know about China anyway? I had never been there; I was never likely to go there; and so on. There's one sure thing about arguing with God—He always wins! Within a couple of months I was in China.

"It is almost impossible for anyone who has not lived and worked in China to understand the actual situation there, much less to write a book about the subject!" That was the pointed comment made to me by a "China expert" on learning that I was writing this book. I had to agree, although I felt like saying, "You had better take that up with God." In fact, as soon as I had come to terms with what God was asking me to do, I began to understand what was to be the nature of the book.

In order to explain something of what is happening now in China, it has proved necessary to give a brief outline of China's history—how the church was planted, and how it has fared under communism. However, I have come to see that what has been happening in mainland China has significance, not for that country only, but for the church of God worldwide, especially in the West. It seemed that God was there writing up, in bold Chinese characters, things

that He wanted me to convey to His people in the free world.
They concern truths of great importance as this present age
moves on to its climax.

Just to handle the material has done something for me. I
can never be quite the same again. Often my manuscript has
been wet with tears—not tears of sadness or sentimentality
or sympathy, but of awe, of wonder, of sheer admiration for
the grace of God at work in mortal flesh. Out of the melting
has come worship. My God, how great you are! If others'
hearts are also melted as they read—not to cool and solidify
again in the old mold, but to be poured into a new mold of
God's choosing—the book will have accomplished its aim.

2

HEIGHTS AND DEPTHS

*For I am convinced that neither death
nor life, neither angels nor demons,
neither the present nor the future . . .
neither height nor depth, nor anything
else in all creation, will be able to
separate us from the love of God that is
in Christ Jesus our Lord.*

Romans 8:38-39

China is the oldest civilization in the world. In its long and
turbulent history spanning fifty centuries, it has scaled the
heights of success and achievement, and has plummeted to
the depths of defeat and humiliation. Excavations in north
central China uncovered a highly developed civilization,
with its own written language, that existed almost 2,000
years before Christ. About the time of Moses (1500 B.C.) the
Chinese were wearing furs and silks, producing beautiful
works of art, erecting elaborate buildings, and going to war
in wheeled chariots. In 1000 B.C. they had a national
university in their capital city, and were using a compass to
chart their journeys.

It was the Qin (Ch'in)[1] dynasty (255-206 B.C.) that gave
the nation its name China, and its first Emperor, Qin
Shihuang. He in turn gave China its first unified written
language. It would seem that Chairman Mao Zedong (Tse-
tung) drew inspiration for many of his ideas from this
powerful and successful ruler. Shihuang built the Great
Wall as a barricade against the nomadic barbarians who
lived on the borders of China. Some sections had been built
earlier, but he linked them all together and constructed
guard towers every few hundred yards. It was built largely
by slave labor, and thousands of the workers perished in the

course of its construction. Stretching for 1,500 miles along the western border of China, it was built of stone, brick, and earth, was twenty feet in height, had a road on top fifteen feet wide, and was garrisoned by a quarter of a million soldiers.

For more than 3,600 years China was ruled by a succession of dynasties. The Ming dynasty (1368-1644) was especially famous for its architecture, furniture, paintings, and pottery. Not far from where I used to live in the southwest of England, a representative of Sotheby's, the famous auctioneers, spotted a small porcelain jar serving as a flowerpot in a lady's garden. He advised her to have it valued. It was found to be a very rare fifteenth century Imperial Ming. It was subsequently auctioned for a modest quarter of a million pounds!

It was China, with its great love of learning and scholarship, that gave us paper in A.D. 105 and the first dictionary, with 10,000 characters. So great was Chinese respect for learning that for centuries they would never throw away a piece of paper with writing on it. It had to be burned in a special receptacle. In Britain the use of fingerprints as a method of identification goes back to about 1880. The Chinese use of them for this purpose goes back to A.D. 700! About A.D. 1000 they invented gunpowder, used at first to make firecrackers to scare off evil spirits. During this period they also discovered a vaccine for smallpox and produced the first reference book on medicine. The Chinese certainly made a unique contribution to the progress of civilization, especially in its earliest centuries.

"Zhongguo," the Chinese word for China, means "the middle country." In Chinese thinking, China is "the middle," the center of the world. Beyond its borders were the inferior races—the outsiders and the barbarians. This national pride and self-centeredness caused them to disdain all that was going on in the big developing world outside. When Lord Macartney, eager to find a market in China for British goods, headed a diplomatic mission to the Manchu Emperor in 1793, he received a cool reception. The Emperor sent a letter to King George III: "As your ambassador can see for himself, we possess all things. I set no value on objects strange or ingenious, and have no use for your country's manufactures."

Confucianism was another factor in China's isolationist policy. A philosophy more than a religion, it had for centuries bred in the Chinese an attitude of resistance to change. All this, together with an inborn fear and hatred of foreigners, from whom they had suffered much, had cut China off from the rest of the world. Consequently she got left behind in the race of human progress. At the beginning of the 1800s China was still a closed land. However, it was soon to be forced open in a way that would leave this proud and cultured nation shamed and humiliated. For this the Western powers, and Britain in particular, must bear the prime responsibility. It is a phase of colonial history which we may prefer to forget. Here seeds were sown which were to bear fruit in the rise and triumph of Chinese Marxism.

The Portuguese were the first to see the potential of marketing Chinese goods in Europe. They secured an island off the coast of China, called Macao, which they still hold. Early in the eighteenth century opium smoking was becoming a social menace in China, through the drug being smuggled into the country from India and Turkey. Portugal saw how this lucrative though immoral trade could be the means of financing her exports to Europe.

It was not long before Britain too saw the trade potential of Chinese goods in Europe. In response to British overtures, China had made it clear that she was not interested in buying British goods, now flowing from the industrial revolution. If China did not want her exports, how could Britain finance the purchase of Chinese tea and silks? Only, it would seem, by following the despicable example of the Portuguese and getting involved in opium smuggling. All this was done with the knowledge and connivance of the British government.

Through the powerful East India Trading Company, operating under the patronage of the British government, the illegal traffic greatly increased, to the alarm of the Chinese government. The British parliament seemed to have no qualms about trading opium, at least not to the Chinese. It was only the smuggling aspect of it that seemed

to trouble the British conscience. It needed to be legalized.
But the Chinese were not interested in negotiating a free-
trade agreement. They were fighting to curb this nefarious
traffic that was bringing such misery to their people.

When the Chinese adopted a get-tough policy, the British
navy became involved, and fighting broke out. China was to
pay dearly for daring to resist the exploitation of her people.
It took two Opium Wars to finally bring China to her knees.
The first was concluded in 1842 with the Treaty of Nanking.
This required China to surrender to the British the island of
Hong Kong and to permit foreigners to reside, for the
purpose of trade or other legitimate activities, in the five
"treaty ports" on the China coast. These foreigners were to
have special rights. They could only be tried for criminal
offenses by courts composed of their own nationals, not by
Chinese courts of law—a terrible humiliation for the Chinese
nation.

The second Opium War, which broke out in 1856, ended
with the sacking of Beijing by European troops and the
signing of the Treaty of Tientsin in 1860. This gave Britain
further territory on the mainland opposite Hong Kong,
called the New Territories (which are due to be returned to
China, together with the island of Hong Kong, in 1997). In
addition, further treaty ports were to be opened; there was to
be freedom for foreigners to travel anywhere in China; and
the opium trade was legalized. The "Unequal Treaties," as
they came to be called, were deeply resented. This was the
beginning of the rape of China by the West.

If Britain was the main culprit in doing the "dirty work,"
the other major powers must share her guilt. As China lay
prostrate and bleeding, they gathered round to take their
share of the spoil. It is not without significance that the first
shots of the Opium War were fired by British naval ships on
the Chinese war junks between Hong Kong and Kowloon, on
the mainland, two territories that are shortly to be handed
back to mainland China.   Again, it is not without
significance that the Western nations that so greedily
participated in illegal drug trafficking now have a drug
problem of massive proportions that they cannot control.
"You reap what you sow" is true of nations as well as of
individuals.

Another unfortunate aspect of the opium racket was the fact that the first Protestant missionaries to China were from the same nation, Britain, that was condoning opium smuggling. It was only through the good offices of the British East India Company that Western missionaries could at first gain entry into the country. So, in the minds of many Chinese, "foreign devils" (Westerners), "foreign mud" (as they called opium), and foreign religion were all of a piece.

Writing from the Chinese port of Swatow in 1856, Hudson Taylor, the pioneer missionary, recounted the following: "Not less than 32,000 pounds of opium enter China every month at this port alone, the cost of which is about a quarter of a million sterling. After this you will not be surprised to learn that the people are wretchedly poor, ignorant and vicious." Later he wrote, not surprisingly, "The people have no love for foreigners."

It was throughout this traumatic period of Chinese history that those early Christian pioneers were laying the foundations of the church in China. "The caliber of these early missionaries was often of the highest order. Scholars, linguists, doctors and teachers came using their skills, thus preparing the way for the spread of the gospel."[2] We must salute these heralds of the cross, who at enormous sacrifice—sometimes of life itself—blazed a trail right into the heart of China. Later we will consider the strengths and weaknesses of the early missionary movement in light of what is now taking place, but their dedication and self-sacrifice can never be questioned.

The dawn of the twentieth century found China weak and vulnerable. The incursions of the West had greatly weakened her, and after centuries of isolation she was in no way ready to take her place alongside other world powers. The Imperial Manchu government, the dynasty that had ruled China for 260 years, was inefficient and corrupt. It came to an end when the Emperor was forced to resign in 1911.

The years that followed the formation of a republican government in China proved to be tempestuous ones, witnessing radical changes and preparing the way for the establishment of the People's Republic of China in 1949.

If we are to have an understanding of the two kingdoms, one temporal and the other eternal, that are now vying for the hearts of the Chinese, we must look more carefully at this fascinating and formative thirty-eight year period. We may be surprised to discover that at the very inception of the Chinese Republic there were strong Christian as well as socialist influences at work. Let us take a few pages, then, to look back at the seedbed of the Communist Revolution.

3

THE SKY IS RED

It is God who judges; He brings one down, he exalts another.

Psalm 75:7

While dynastic rule was in its death throes, a leader appeared on the political scene with the vision of a China strong and free. Dr. Sun Yat-sen, although Chinese-born, had spent much of his youth in Hawaii. He had traveled widely both in America and Europe. He had been influenced not only by the principles of parliamentary democracy, but by the socialist ideas of men like Karl Marx as well. He had a consuming passion to see a free and prosperous China, and his fertile mind was ever searching for answers to the nation's urgent social and economic problems. Although he had no prior experience or training in government, he was dedicated to the overthrow of the Manchu Dynasty.

Traveling overseas, Sun raised funds from Chinese expatriates, and was involved in several abortive attempts to overthrow the Imperial government. A high price was placed on his head. The climate was ripe for change, if not for revolution. Most Chinese were convinced that the government was corrupt, but few had any clear idea of the right course to take.

As a politician, Sun was something of a hybrid. He was committed to constitutional democracy while holding socialist ideas on land reform and the regulation of capital. Probably his vision was to combine a democratic form of government with socialist principles for the economy. Consequently Dr. Sun Yat-sen is acclaimed by the Nationalists as the instigator of democracy in China, and by the Communists as their first revolutionary. A revolutionary he was, but not a Marxist. "The reason the revolution succeeded," he declared, "was because I relied totally on God's help." That is not the confession of a Marxist.

Dr. Sun was evidently a committed Christian. In 1912, speaking in a church in Boston, Mass., he declared,

> Men say that the revolution originated with me. I do not deny the charge. But where did the idea of revolution come from? It came because, from my youth, I was brought in touch with foreign missionaries. Those from Europe and America with whom I associated put the ideals of freedom and liberty in my heart. Now I call upon the church to help in the establishment of the new government. The Republic cannot endure unless there is that virtue, righteousness, at the center of the nation's life.

In a letter to old friends of his in Hong Kong, he wrote on the occasion of his election to the presidency, "I thank you for your earnest prayers on my behalf. I am glad to tell you that we are going to have religious toleration in China, and I assure you that Christianity will flourish under the new regime." Dr. Sun's son, a number of his cabinet colleagues, and his private secretary were all committed Christians. It was amazing to find that the gospel of Christ had penetrated to the highest levels of government.

October 10, 1911, called in China the "Double Tenth," is still viewed as the birth of the Revolution. An army unit revolted, the Imperial palace was attacked, and not long afterward the Emperor abdicated. Dr. Sun,who was overseas raising funds, hurried back to China, and on New Year's Day 1912 was inaugurated as the first president of the Republic.

Sun's initial tenure of office was very brief. A power struggle followed his election, and he was ousted. Control in China fell into the hands of a number of warlords. It was not until ten years later that Sun was able to grasp again the reins of leadership.

Meanwhile a series of events had taken place that were to have a profound effect on China in shaping the type of government that would come out of the Chinese melting pot. The first of these events took place in Russia in 1917: it was the Bolshevik Revolution. Initially this had little impact on China. The new Republican government was not looking to Russia for answers.

The next event came with the conclusion of World War I, in which China had sided with the Allies. On the conclusion of hostilities (1918) she was fully expecting that Chinese territory held by Germany would be restored to her. Assurances to this effect had been given by Woodrow Wilson, the American president. Eventually—when the Versailles Treaty was concluded in 1919—this territory was given to Japan, who had captured it from the Germans during the war.

This was a devastating blow to China, and produced deep resentment and widespread political reaction. For many Chinese, faith in democracy and the West was shattered, and many eyes were turned toward Russia and the Bolshevik Revolution for a solution to China's problems. Russia was more than willing to respond by moving into the vacuum created by the Treaty of Versailles. Marxism became Russia's big export to China, and Comintern agents were trained in Moscow to incite rebellion and to form Communist cells. It was as a result of this activity that in 1921 the Chinese Communist Party was formed.

A nationalist fervor now took over, one that China had never witnessed before. Two forces emerged, each making its bid to lead the nation into a new day of prosperity and liberty. One advocated democracy, science, and modern education, and called for the renunciation of the ancient traditional culture. The other, finding its inspiration in the Bolshevik Revolution, believed that Marxism was the answer. Both now turned to Sun Yat-sen as the only man who could harmonize these two conflicting ideals and unite the nation. He proposed a democratic form of government that advocated aspects of Marxism in its economic program and the handling of land ownership.

Probably Dr. Sun's greatest miscalculation was to assume that Western democracy could be immediately introduced to China when there was no foundation for it. Professor C.P. Fitzgerald has pointed out that in Chinese thinking, "There is no place for freedom as the West understands it, no place for salvation as the Christian understands it, and no place for individualism as the liberal would have it." Given time, there was little doubt which way the pendulum would swing.

Dr. Sun's reelection to the presidency in 1922 was short-lived. He died in 1925. The conflicting ideologies to which he had been subjected, some of which he had embraced, never robbed him of his faith. On his death bed he declared, "I am a disciple of Jesus Christ, commissioned by God to declare war against evil. Even when I die, I want people to know I am a Christian."

A young army officer who also possessed Christian convictions had become Sun's right hand man. His name was Chiang Kai-shek. He had been to Moscow, and like Sun had been initially influenced by Marxism. Dr. Sun's mantle now came to rest on him. The Nationalist Kuomintang government that he now headed decided to continue Sun's policies. The situation that they faced was not just one of change, or of transition, but of revolution, and the tasks for the new government were enormous.

By 1927, though the Nationalists had broken with the Communists, they had made considerable progress in reunifying the country. Then Mao Zedong marshalled his peasant army, based at this time in southeast China, and began his famous Long March to the steppes of the northwest. This march, described more fully in the following chapter, is one of the great epics of Chinese history. There he established a secure base from which to conduct his struggle against the Nationalist forces.

It was at this point that a new danger appeared. The Japanese had seized Manchuria and were now threatening China. War with Japan broke out in 1937 and dragged on for eight weary years. The need was urgent for Nationalists and Communists to stand against the common foe. Each accused the other of not doing so. At Mao's instigation they buried the hatchet for the time being, at least, and concentrated on resisting the foreign invader. China was eventually saved by the Allies, who defeated Japan in World War II.

In 1946 civil war between the Nationalists and the Communists broke out in earnest. It was a life and death struggle, lasting from 1946 to 1949, and costing more lives, it is reckoned, than any war of modern times. Slowly and inexorably the Communists pushed back the numerically superior Nationalist forces until they had all been driven from mainland China to find refuge in Taiwan. Then, on a bleak February morning in 1949, the Communist divisions marched into Beijing, and the crimson flag with its five stars was unfurled. Soon after, China's new ruler, Chairman Mao Zedong, proclaimed from the Gate of Heavenly Peace in Beijing the birth of the People's Republic of China.

4

THE GREAT HELMSMAN

*All men are like grass, and all their
glory is like the flowers of the field. The
grass withers and the flowers fall,
because the breath of the Lord blows on
them ... but the word of our God stands
forever.*

Isaiah 40:6-8

We cannot really understand China today without looking
at the man who, more than any other, has shaped the nation.
Mao Zedong was rightly called the "Great Helmsman." To
the young revolutionaries of China he embodied all the
ideals of the Revolution, and they venerated him as though
he were God. Whatever we may think of his political
philosophy and his ruthless methods, no one can deny the
magnitude of his achievement in uniting and galvanizing a
dismembered and dispirited nation—the largest on the face
of the earth—giving them pride in their nationhood, giving
them a universal simplified script, and bringing them "out of
the Middle Ages into the nuclear era" as one of the foremost
Communist states of the twentieth century.

Disillusioned with Western liberalism, Mao embraced
Marxism, which he proceeded to adapt to the Chinese
situation. It was his conviction that China must find its own
form of Marxism. He was one of the twelve founding
members of the Chinese Communist party formed in 1921,
although not at that time the leader. When Chiang Kai-shek
took over leadership of the government on the death of Sun
Yat-sen, Mao cooperated at first with the new leader, but
there was no prospect of any lasting alliance. While
promoting a united front with Chiang, the Communists had

other plans afoot. They began to organize a peasant army of Communist guerillas (1924-25). When the inevitable break came with Chiang, they knew that they had to build up their forces, or the superior Nationalist army would overwhelm them.

Based at that time in southeastern China, the Communists decided to make a strategic retreat to the mountains of the northwest. This involved a trek of some 6,000 miles and the crossing of eighteen mountain ranges and twenty-four rivers. The trek lasted from 1934 to 1936. Throughout this incredible journey, known as the Long March, the Communist forces were constantly harassed by the Nationalists and their numbers greatly reduced through sickness and casualties. Even today, the Chinese consider the feat of the Long March to be one of the proudest moments in their history. It inspired many young Chinese to join the Communist party.

It was during this march that Mao's position as the leader of the Communists was established. At this point he decided to break away from his dependence on Stalin and to plow his own furrow. Having reached his objective, Mao set up his new revolutionary base. The following year Mao's systematic studies of Marxist philosophy began to be published. Later his followers were to describe him as "the greatest genius of our time," and *Mao's Thoughts* as "the greatest truth ever known since time immemorial." In a two year period two billion copies of his writings rolled off the press. This all helped in the deification of Mao. Yet with his decline and death, the Mao legend was to fade and wither like the flower of the field.

The ultimate victory of the Communists over Chiang Kai-shek's forces in 1949 was a tremendous feat, achieved against all odds. Perhaps the major reason was that the Communists had a vision, a cause and an ideal that they felt was worth fighting for and worth dying for. The Nationalists did not. The Communists were excited about their vision, they had faith in its fulfillment, and so they went about seeking to "convert" others to their cause. (Here is an obvious lesson for professing Christians.)

China is essentially a peasant nation tied to tradition,

especially that of Confucianism. There was a strong bond
between ruler and subject, father and son, husband and wife.
Although Mao set himself to improve the lot of the peasants,
he felt that these bonds, together with those of religion,
capitalism, and autocracy, were the major obstacles to
establishing a new Marxist society, and so he set out to
destroy them.

Such radical social changes are seldom effected without
violent conflict. Mao not only accepted this, it was a vital
element in his Communist philosophy. "Revolution is an act
of violence whereby one class overthrows the authority of
another. Revolution is not a dinner party."

Mao was a great visionary and revolutionary thinker, but
he was no economist. To him the important thing was to
maintain the revolutionary spirit, and to abide by his own
Marxist dogmas. Whether the things he had initiated were
really workable seemed only a secondary consideration. In
the years that followed he embarked upon a series of
adventurous policies, all of which proved more or less
disastrous. This undermined people's confidence, as well as
resulting in a great deal of suffering and bitterness.

In the years 1950-52, Mao commenced to wipe out the
landlord class. This involved the liquidation of an estimated
800,000 people and the giving of their land to the peasants.
In 1958 the land was taken from them for state-owned
communes. These could encompass several towns with up to
100,000 people in each. Private ownership was ended and all
was centrally organized. This experiment was something of
a disaster, and the communes have now been dismantled in
China.

The next policy was the "Hundred Flowers" movement in
1956, in which Mao encouraged intellectuals to criticize
government policy. The party was shocked by the strength
and outspokenness of the response. This led to an immediate
crackdown on the intellectuals. Many of them were shipped
to Mongolia, the "Siberia" of China, to Tibet and other
remote regions, and some of them were never heard from
again. Criticism of the government became an act of high
treason. This about-face was another severe blow to the
people's confidence in the integrity of Mao and his policies.

Then came the Great Leap Forward in 1958. Its purpose was to turn China into a vast industrial-agricultural nation that would be able to compete with the major nations of the world. In his attempt to produce "instant success," Mao planned to break up the family unit, which had always been the great strength of the Chinese society. Families were divided up and sent off to form communes. Such a vast undertaking could never be accomplished overnight, and the Great Leap was doomed to failure from the start. Two successive years of drought and flooding sealed its fate. According to Chinese government admission ten million peasants died in the famine. U.S. statistics reckon it was twenty million. At this point Mao became a target for strong criticism within the party.

After a period in semi-seclusion, the Great Helmsman's revolutionary spirit began to stir again. Was he afraid that power was slipping from his hands for good? He was certainly afraid of "revisionism"—that the nation would lose its revolutionary spirit and slide back into moderation and liberalization. Behind the backs of the men in power he planned to make a personal comeback, to mobilize the youth, and to revive the revolutionary spirit. This movement came to be called the Great Cultural Revolution; it proved to be the biggest disaster of all.

Bypassing both the army and the party, neither of which he could fully trust, Mao took his case directly to the youth of the country. He ordered all schools to be closed. He addressed a million Red Guards in Beijing, commissioning them to travel through the nation destroying old ideas, customs, and habits, crushing all who were thought to be taking the capitalist road.

The revolution almost became a riot. Houses were looted, the elderly abused, and innocent people condemned. To denounce someone as a capitalist was an easy way to settle old scores. The young Red Guards were often totally undisciplined. It is said that a million illegitmate babies were born during this period. Priceless art treasures were destroyed. Churches, even those operating under the authority of the government, and all other religious buildings were closed. The Chinese church went through a winter of desolation. There was soon a strong reaction against the ruthless behavior of these young revolutionaries. Rival groups sprang up within the Red Guard movement. Pitched battles occurred and a general state of disorder prevailed.

Meanwhile farming had been neglected and the economy was moving towards a precipice of disaster. Mao admitted that the Red Guards had not fulfilled his high expectations of them, and the army was called in to restore order.

The revolution had by now touched the highest echelons of government. Even President Liu Shaoqi, Mao's appointed successor, was publicly humiliated and branded a "lackey of imperialism." He was dismissed from the party and died in prison some years later.

The Red Guards were dedicated to boosting the image of Mao to the point where he was virtually deified. At first they erected his portrait in every public place. They waved the "Little Red Book" and chanted Mao's thoughts. But when the reaction set in, all this began to disappear from the scene. Mao's young henchmen had thoroughly discredited him. Many of them were sent home in disgrace or were sent away to work on communes. In the words of a distinguished Communist party writer, "The Great Cultural Revolution was the greatest revolution that sent culture to its death." It is doubtful whether Mao's image in the thinking of the Chinese people ever recovered from this debacle.

Contemporary with Mao was another man who made a notable contribution to the shaping of the People's Republic—Zhou Enlai (Chou En-lai). He was appointed premier when the Republic was founded in 1949, a position which he held until his death a few months before that of Mao. An outstanding diplomat, highly respected internationally and loved by the Chinese people, he acted to restrain the extremists in the Cultural Revolution. It was largely through his diplomatic initiative that China was admitted to the United Nations in 1971. It was he who invited the U.S. to send a table-tennis team to China—"Ping Pong Diplomacy"—which led to the visit of President Nixon and the eventual resumption of diplomatic relations with America.

The difference in the political outlook of Mao and Zhou became all too clear in their later years. It represented a tension that is reflected today in the struggle for power within the Chinese Communist party. It is the conflict between the leftists, or dogmatists, and the pragmatists. Mao was a dogmatist, wedded to Marxism, from which there could be no deviation. His ideology blinded him to the fact that his theories were not working and would never work. Zhou, on the other hand, was a pragmatist, with his feet firmly on the ground. If a political theory was not producing results it must be modified or scrapped.

The pragmatists see no hope of China ever competing with the major nations of the world without the easing of controls and "modernization." There must be freedom for initiative and enterprise. Workers need more than revolutionary ideals; they must have financial incentives if output is to increase. The nation needs modernizing if its vast resources are to be harnessed to the building of a strong and prosperous China. That means opening the country to the techniques and expertise of the West.

The leftists see these trends as highly dangerous. When the people get a taste of liberty and prosperity, they no longer turn up at Party meetings to study Marxism. They lose their revolutionary zeal. To allow the people to fraternize freely with foreigners would open them to the decadent influences of the West. The Party would lose its tight control over the people. The nation would slide back into capitalism.

These opposing viewpoints are reflected in the slogan of the pragmatists, "It doesn't matter what color the cat is, as long as it catches mice," and in the retort of the leftists, "It doesn't matter if the cat catches mice or not, as long as it is red!" This is the dilemma now facing Chinese communism.

In July 1976 the "Great Helmsman" died, leaving a dispirited and disillusioned nation. Here are the words of a youth by the name of Mo-min, who wrote in one of China's newspapers:

> The word "tomorrow" has been a word of great fascination to me. When I was attending primary school, the Great Leap Forward was the dream of tomorrow; we were going to live happily in prosperity.

But what did we get? Disasters!
And then The Cultural Revolution: tomorrow means
total liberation, and we shall conquer the world. What
did we get? Disasters! Now the young people of China
cannot help but learn this lesson: Don't hope too much!
Don't be optimistic! Don't think about tomorrow!

Here are the concluding remarks on Mao by an able student
of the China scene: "If he had died some twenty-five years
earlier, he would most certainly have gone down in Chinese
history as one of the greatest Chinese reformers. As it was,
he lived long enough to thoroughly destroy his own hard-
won reputation."[3]

On his deathbed Mao appointed Hua Guofeng as his
successor, although in fact the power was already in the
hands of the "Gang of Four." This consisted of his widow,
Jiang Qing (Chiang Ch'ing)—who had her sights set on the
chairmanship—and her three colleagues. How much this
was the result of Mao's connivance, and how much due to the
fact that he was too old to do anything about it, is not clear;
but in the eyes of many Chinese, Mao's crowning failure was
his inability to restrain his ambitious wife. As one writer put
it, "Without Mao, there would have been no Madame Mao."
The suspicion of Mao's complicity was expressed in one of
the famous wall posters that spoke of the "Gang of Five"!

It was this group of political schemers that dominated the
closing years of the Mao era. In the period of unrest that
followed the Chairman's death, the Gang of Four was
arrested and eventually tried and imprisoned. The leader
who eventually emerged was Deng Xiaoping. Though he
declined to take the official position of chairman or premier,
preferring to lead from behind, he was clearly the new strong
man of China. He now began to turn the nation in a
completely new direction. He introduced the "Four
Modernizations" program, aimed at agriculture, industry,
defense, and science.

From 1978 it seemed that even the Bamboo Curtain was
lifting. China entered a phase of liberty that it had not
enjoyed since the Communists came to power. Foreign
guests became a familiar sight in the streets of China's
major cities. Young Chinese were able to go overseas to

study. Business enterprises sprang up. People called it the "Second Liberation."

A wall in Beijing became world-famous as posters were plastered up that in a subtle way disclosed the thinking of many Chinese regarding the "feudalism" of the Mao era and the longing for greater freedom. It is said that Deng Xiaoping instigated the Big Poster Campaign on "Democracy Wall." However, this opportunity for free expression went "overboard" (according to the government), and the leadership was compelled to put a stop to what could have become a popular revolt.

Deng's progressive economic measures came into serious trouble. Also, his liberalization was thought to be resulting in too much crime, opening the nation to the decadence of the West. So, early in the eighties, the pendulum began to swing the other way, in one of those reversals of policy which the Chinese have learned to expect. Thankfully there was no return to the savage oppression of the Cultural Revolution. Nevertheless there was a significant tightening of control in a way typical of a Marxist state.

Deng now launched the "Anti-Crime Campaign," resulting in an estimated 100,000 arrests and 10,000 executions. This was followed by the "Anti-Spiritual Pollution Campaign," aimed at countering liberalizing tendencies, especially those coming in from outside. This became in some quarters an excuse for attacking the unofficial house churches. Finally there was the "Party Rectification Campaign," which appeared to be Deng's effort to purge from the Party those who held strong leftist positions so that he could proceed with pragmatic policies.

What of the future? The most knowledgeable are wisely the most reluctant to predict. Deng is in his eighties. He may no longer be around by the time you read this. Who will follow him, and in what direction will he lead China? How reassuring to know that these decisions are not in fact in the hands of man. "The authorities that exist have been established by God."[4]

The reader will be eager to know how all this has affected and is affecting the church of Jesus Christ. First, we must go back and see how the church was planted in China and how it has been faring in a Marxist society.

5

PLANTING THE CHURCH

*The kingdom of heaven is like a mustard
seed, which a man took and planted in
his field. Though it is the smallest of all
your seeds, yet when it grows, it is the
largest of garden plants and becomes a
tree, so that the birds of the air come and
perch in its branches.*
Matthew 13:31-32

The first to sow the seeds of Christianity in China were
Nestorians who came from Persia and built churches and
monasteries. Later came Catholic missionaries. They did
not preach a truly saving message and never succeeded in
making the faith indigenous to China. With the overthrow
of the Mongols, Christianity was "sunk almost without
trace."

In 1579 the Roman Catholic church made a fresh attempt
to establish the faith in China. Jesuit missionaries came
from the Portuguese colony of Macao just off the southern
coast of China. Eventually, when they took a stand against
ancestor worship, they were forbidden by the Emperor to
preach. There was a mass exodus of priests, and again the
light of the Christian faith was all but extinguished.

In 1807 Robert Morrison, a young Scot with the London
Missionary Society, set sail for China with a burning desire
to lead the Chinese people to Christ. The problem was how to
gain entry, since the British East India Company was the
doorkeeper, and was scared of missionary activity affecting
its trade with China. Eventually Morrison arrived in
Macao, where he settled down to translate the Scriptures
into Chinese, a task which he finally accomplished some
eighteen years later. The problem with this translation, as

well as that of another by a Dr. Marshman, was that it was
in the classical style used by scholars but not understood by
the common people.   Nevertheless, both the translations
were a tremendous achievement of missionary endeavor.

Later, after some hesitation, Morrison accepted an
appointment as translator to the East India Company
simply to gain entrance to his beloved China.   Thus it was
that Christian missionaries and the iniquitous opium trade
carried on by the East India Company were to be forever
linked in the minds of the Chinese.   As we have seen, the two
treaties of 1842 and 1860 forced China to open her doors to
the West, both for free trade and for missionary activity.

The China Inland Mission under the leadership of
Hudson Taylor, as well as other missionary agencies, had
been newly formed.   In the years that followed, first a trickle
and then a swelling stream of dedicated missionaries came
to China from the West.   Those early servants of God in
China were not to know that in less than a hundred years
every Christian missionary would be evacuated from the
mainland, with little prospect of the door reopening.   The
church of Jesus Christ that they established in that land was
to go through its baptism of fire, testing to the utmost the
quality of the work, and revealing its strengths and its
weaknesses.

There is no question as to the dedication of those early
missionaries and the tremendous sacrifices they gladly
made for the cause of Christ.   Many of them were highly
trained and gifted.   Of all nations, the Chinese set a high
value on scholarship and culture, and this worked in favor of
the early missionary effort.   In other respects, however,
events weighed heavily against them.   In the beginning they
had gained entry, as we have already seen, through the
discredited colonial policies of Britain and the West.   It has
been said, "Opium traffic was the single greatest
impediment to Christianity in China in the nineteenth
century."

Having experienced for centuries the cruelty of the
foreign invader, the Chinese looked upon the activity of all
foreigners with the greatest suspicion.   No wonder the
ambassador of the cross was viewed as a "foreign devil," and

any Chinese who embraced his doctrine as a "half-foreigner." This whole attitude was to strengthen the arm of the Communists when they came to power determined to drive out all foreign missionaries from the land. They did not need to think up a "case" against foreign missionaries. The colonial policies of Britain and the West provided them with all the ammunition they required. The fact that the missionaries themselves had been totally opposed to the opium trade and the fact that it was eventually committed Christians in the British parliament who fought successfully to have the traffic stopped, did not absolve Christianity of its guilt in the eyes of the Communists.

On the other side of the coin, poor Chinese, who hadn't much to lose anyway by associating with foreigners, could respond to the gospel for the wrong motives. To them, the missionary was always wealthy, and he occupied a position of privilege in the land. The temptation to be a "rice Christian" who professed faith for material advantage was augmented by the fact that the treaties secured by the West offered benefits for Christian converts.

The other weakness of the early missionary effort, like that of the Nestorian and Catholic enterprises before it, was that it imposed Western forms of worship and culture upon the Chinese, ways that were totally foreign to them. Most of the early missionary organizations failed to see that if the church was ever to root naturally in the soil of China, it needed to be divested of its Western forms.

Among those early pioneers, Hudson Taylor was the exception in this respect, for he encouraged his missionaries to adopt Chinese dress and to identify in every possible way with the Chinese culture. He sought to raise up national leadership and to hand over the reins to those leaders as soon as they were capable of taking over. But for this he heaped upon himself much abuse and criticism from other missionaries.

Another great weakness was that missionary organizations generally established their churches on denominational lines. The Church of Christ in China was the amalgamation of several denominations, each retaining its own distinctive identity. Even the China Inland Mission, which in so many other respects had adapted to Chinese culture, distributed its workers over the various provinces according to their denominational identity, each church retaining its own particular form of church government. An Anglican bishop was appointed over the Anglican churches. In this way the tragic divisions of Western Christendom were exported to China.

In the period of unrest that marked the closing years of imperial rule, there was a violent outbreak of anti-foreign and anti-missionary feeling: it was the Boxer Rebellion of 1900, which was designed to drive out the foreigner with his political, social, and religious traditions. Although it lasted only a year, its effects were devastating. It almost brought the great missionary venture to a tragic end. Foreigners in large centers were more easily protected; but missionaries, often in isolated places, were particularly vulnerable. Nearly 200 Protestant missionaries and their dependents died, and the Roman Catholic losses were even heavier. Christian leaders among the Chinese suffered greatly, too. There were amazing stories of heroism and loyalty as the Chinese church faced this terrible ordeal. It was a foretaste of what was to happen on a much wider scale when the Communists took over.

With the dawn of the twentieth century we reach a fascinating phase in the story of the planting of the church in China. God is never limited to what we consider "the proper channels." He has His own ways of working. China has a long history of spontaneous and indigenous movements of the Spirit. Some of these revival movements were God's way of cleansing and purifying His people and filling them with the power of the Holy Spirit. It was so with the revivals under the ministry of the Canadian missionary, Jonathan Goforth. These revivals took place first in Manchuria (1908) and were followed by outbreaks in other parts of China.

There were other revivals in which the emphasis was decidedly evangelistic, with powerful preaching of the gospel, and with many turning to Christ. John Sung, whose ministry was not confined to China, was mightily used in the period prior to the Communist takeover. This eccentric preacher was only forty-two when he died, but he turned thousands to Christ. He has been described as "the greatest evangelist China has ever known."

There was the great pastor-preacher Wang Mingdao, who drew thousands to his church in Beijing, and who stood as a bastion of righteousness when other Chinese leaders compromised with the authorities. We shall hear more about him later.

It is significant that before the Communists came to power there were a number of indigenous movements that, in different ways, attempted to restructure and revitalize the body of Christ. They were recovery movements that restored certain aspects of truth—springs breaking out that would eventually flow into and blend with the main stream of the house church movement in China.

The first to gain prominence was the "True Jesus" church established by Paul Wei in Tianjin (Tientsin) and Beijing in the year 1917. These believers emphasized witnessing, tithing, and local church government. They were at home with spiritual gifts—speaking in tongues, exercising healing and deliverance, and other manifestations of God's power. Communal living was also a feature of their lifestyle in the early days. Their churches sprang up throughout China and among Chinese overseas.

By 1949, when the Communists had taken over, their membership was reported to be 125,000. Compare this with the Church of Christ in China, the union of several major denominations already mentioned, with a membership of 196,000 after a hundred years of missionary effort. Denominational structures do not facilitate but rather hinder swift expansion. When churches free themselves from this yoke they tend to make more rapid growth. But there are dangers if a movement becomes exclusive; and the True Jesus church did not escape this hazard, so that later on some excesses and divisions marred their testimony.

Another remarkable movement was that of the "Little Flock," which began in 1926 under the leadership of Watchman Nee, whose Chinese name was Nee To-sheng (the surname being placed first). Through his books, almost all written by others from his sermon notes, he is the most well-known Chinese Christian in the West. For a short time he had association with the "Exclusive Brethren," though he did not initially draw his insight from them. In fact, when he visited one of their churches in Britain and was asked by his host, "What do you think of our assembly?", he replied, "Very nice, very nice, brother," and then shaking his head slowly, he added, "But no good for casting out demons in China!" Watchman Nee and his fellow workers knew the necessity of the empowering of the Holy Spirit.

Nee had no time for formality and "churchianity." He was critical of the current missionary movement and the way in which the Chinese church had become dependent on the West. He took the New Testament, as had many others before him, as providing all the principles needed for New Testament life and practice. He saw the founding of churches as a ministry of apostolic men, who were itinerant and were to be distinguished from the local pastors and teachers.

Nee inevitably drew upon himself a flood of criticism from those in the missionary movement, particularly when some missionaries, and even whole churches founded by missionaries, joined the Little Flock; but his work grew and prospered, even after the Communists had taken over. In twenty years the movement numbered 700 churches with more than 70,000 members.

Some division occurred in the Little Flock shortly before the Communist takeover. After the arrest of Watchman Nee, his colleague, Witness Li—then based in Taiwan—became the dominant leader; but the direction of his leadership did not find accord with many of the Little Flock assemblies, and the movement was split. Li's followers earned the nickname "The Shouters" because of their practice of shouting out en masse in their meetings, "Lord Jesus, Lord Jesus . . ." In China they have been proscribed by the Communists as "counterrevolutionary," a serious charge, and many of their leaders have been imprisoned. Some house church leaders not connected with "The Shouters" have been accused of belonging to them, and have been imprisoned.

The last of these indigenous movements was that of the

"Jesus Family," which was born out of the Shandong
(Shantung) revival in the early 1930s. It was founded by a
converted Buddhist, Ching Tien-ying. With the Scriptures
as his only guidance, Ching built up a fellowship of believers
that eventually spread throughout northern China and deep
into the interior. They were led to structure the church so
that it could function in a Communist environment. They
were deeply involved in agriculture and developed efficient
land policies that brought abundant crops.

They began to give a tenth away to the poor, and when in
1942 there was a great famine, they gave away 20 percent of
their harvest. Before long, they were giving away nine-
tenths and living on one-tenth. On forty-three acres of land
they succeeded in supporting 500 people, and gave away 90
percent of their harvest. The Communists, who boasted of
their land policies, could never compete with the Jesus
Family.

Because the Jesus Family had no central control, would
accept no foreign funds, and set aside no buildings
specifically for church worship, the Communists could not
"nail them" on the usual charges. For this reason they were
able to hold the Communists at bay when many other
churches were shut down. These policies were ones to which
they had been guided by the Holy Spirit twenty years before
the Communists took over.

Born in a revival movement in which manifestations of
the Spirit were normal, Jesus Family meetings included
speaking in tongues, healing, and casting out of demons in
their meetings. In those early years the church had
experiences of angelic ministry and the miraculous supply of
needs.

In pointing out some of the inherent weaknesses of the
missionary movement that planted the church in China, it
must be remembered that those early pioneers were the
spiritual children of their generation. They served God
according to the light they had received, and did so
zealously. We cannot judge them according to the light God
is giving His people a century and a half later.

Much that they built has withstood the wind and the
flood; and, together with all that has come through those

indigenous and spontaneous movements of the Spirit, has found a permanent place in that building of God which is now the church in China. Without their sacrificial sowing *then*, there would be no harvest *now*.

6

THE LONG DARK NIGHT

Why do the nations rage and the peoples plot in vain? The kings of the earth take their stand and the rulers gather together against the Lord and against his Anointed One. "Let us break their chains," they say, "and throw off their fetters." The One enthroned in heaven laughs; the Lord scoffs at them. Then he rebukes them in his anger and terrifies them in his wrath, saying, "I have installed my King on Zion, my holy hill."
Psalm 2:1-6

There are many reasons why God chooses to visit His people with the reviving power of the Holy Spirit. One of these is to prepare them for a time of persecution. It happened in Korea before the country was torn apart by the conflict between North and South that broke out in 1950. It happened in 1953 in Zaire, or the Congo as it was then known, shortly before the terrible bloodbath that followed the declaration of independence. It happened likewise in China immediately preceding the Communist takeover in 1949.

Hundreds of missionaries who had fled the country due to the Sino-Japanese War were now returning. Significant numbers of university students were converted on the campuses and many offered themselves for full-time Christian work. Despite the conflict between the Nationalists and the Communists, from many different areas there came reports of crowded churches, massive Bible conferences, and successful evangelistic campaigns. Indigenous missionary societies came into being; they sent missionaries to the more remote areas. The Bible Society recorded the distribution of three million copies of the

Scriptures in one year. The Bible had become China's best seller.

Missionaries and other church leaders were gratified to observe that there was no looting or raping by the advancing Communist troops, nor was any immediate pressure put on the city churches. This was other than what they had been led to expect, so they pressed on with their appointed work. If some church leaders were fooled by this initial friendliness and affability of the Communists, leading evangelicals like Watchman Nee and Wang Mingdao were not. They had discerned the true nature of the Communist movement and knew that the leopard does not change its spots.

It is not difficult to see why the Communists adopted this strategy. In the first place, they did not want to antagonize Christians before they were secure in their rulership. Second, they needed the expertise of many of the Christians, who were among the most capable members of the community. Finally, the strategy provided an opportunity for them to observe and take stock of the churches, and especially the church leaders.

By mid-1950 the Communist rulers had set in motion a plan designed to eliminate the influence of Christianity throughout the country. Step one was to bring the professing church under their control. They persuaded a number of Chinese church leaders to sign certain documents acknowledging that "Christianity, consciously or unconsciously, directly or indirectly, related to imperialism." It was a fact of history that Christian missions had received great benefit from Western imperialist policies in China. Chinese leaders were now persuaded by Communist propaganda that the Chinese church must be totally free of Western support and control. The Communist slogan, "Love country—love church," in that order, took off.

We see here the subtlety of the Communists in making use of scriptural teaching and even Christian catch phrases, which they subverted to their own purposes. Watchman Nee was strong on the oneness of the body of Christ, that it was not to be segmented into different denominations. Some missionaries had already begun to teach that local churches should be self-governing, self-supporting, and self-propagating. This became the slogan of the Communists. Their idea was to isolate the church from all outside influence, especially from that of the West. Once the church was united under a central organization and totally cut off from the West, it would be easy for the Party to control it. If it did not die a natural death, it could be rendered harmless.

This is the Communist thinking behind the forming of an "official church," controlled by the state, called the "Three-Self Patriotic Movement." "Patriotic" expresses the idea of "Love country—love church," and "Three-Self" the policy of being self-governing, self-supporting, and self-propagating. This Party propaganda put many church leaders into a state of inner conflict. They wanted to be loyal to their country, but they had a "gut feeling" that state control would in the long run be detrimental to the interests of the kingdom of God. It was a repeat of the crucial issue that faced those first-century Christians. Who is lord—Caesar or Christ?

Missionaries now faced the agonizing decision to stay put or to pull out. The Communists did not issue an official edict, but it was abundantly clear that the new regime did not want the missionaries. The deciding question had to be, "What is best for the Chinese church?" The Protestant societies rightly judged that their continued presence would only embarrass and hamper the Chinese believers. Accordingly they gave the order to evacuate, and by early 1952 all missionaries except the Roman Catholics had left the country.

Every branch of the Christian church now came under severe pressure. This was reflected in the sharp decline in attendance and membership in all the major denominations. By contrast, in those years from 1949 to 1957, the indigenous churches—that is, those that were not the product of Western missionary activity, but had sprung up from the native soil of China—made quite dramatic gains, their numbers almost tripling. Many of the new members were believers who were leaving their churches, now under the Three-Self Patriotic Movement, as they discovered the political overtones of the new organization.

The Communists then embarked on an aggressive

campaign to vilify prominent leaders, especially those who were evangelical. It was not too difficult to bring into line denominations and para-church organizations which had central control, but the indigenous churches were proving to be a much more difficult proposition. In 1951 the son of the founder of the Jesus Movement was imprisoned. The following year Jing Tianying of the Jesus Family and Watchman Nee of the Little Flock were arrested and sentenced. And in 1955 the same fate at last overtook the courageous Wang Mingdao.

Those arrested were subjected to the usual Communist brainwashing techniques. The aim was to break the will of the prisoner and compel him to submit to Marxist dogma. He needed to be reeducated. He was required to survey his past life in detail, to confess his guilt against the state, to repent and achieve a state of atonement—a perverted and humanistic form of "salvation." Many stood firm through the ordeal, but others caved in.

Wang Mingdao had been a constant thorn in the side of the Communists. At first the authorities had difficulty finding a charge against him. He had refused to attend seminary, feeling it was missionary-dominated, and had never been ordained or supported financially by foreign missionaries. Like Nee, he had been fairly critical of much Western missionary effort. His only education for the ministry had come from the Holy Spirit. As a man of God, the Communists could find no fault in him.

His church, the largest in Beijing, was always packed, and often there would be 1,000 or more outside to whom the word was relayed by loudspeaker. It could be that he preached to more Chinese than any other man. He was uncompromising on sin and proclaimed a thoroughly evangelical message. When eventually he was brought to public trial, his whole congregation was forced to attend. He was charged with being anti-government and anti-Three-Self movement and with preaching irregular messages. One quarter of the Christians and others present, as a result of official church pressure, called for the death sentence. He was given no opportunity to speak in self-defense, but so strong was public feeling in his favor that the authorities were forced to release him.

Later, when he was again brought to trial, although he never spoke against the regime, Wang was fearless in his criticism of the theologically liberal clergy and those in the Three-Self movement, whom he accused of betraying Christ. He was given a fifteen year prison sentence and was immediately subjected to the Communist reeducation process. Two shifts of political experts worked on him day and night. After thirteen months of mental torture he broke and signed a confession. He was required to read this publicly to a large audience. His capitulation made headlines on the page of every newspaper: "I am an anti-revolutionary criminal. I am grateful to the government for pardoning me and saving me from the depths of sin...," and so on.

A few days after his release he was seen walking up and down the streets of Beijing shouting, "I am Judas, I have betrayed my Lord." In fact his confession did not involve a denial of Christ. A few days later when the equilibrium of his mind was restored, he went with his wife to the government authorities and retracted his confession. "Imprison me if you will," he said, "but I will not betray my Lord." He was immediately sent back to prison together with his wife and there this courageous man of God spent the next twenty-two years, to be released in 1980 at the age of eighty.

Experiences of this kind were repeated over and over in the history of the Chinese church in Red China. Many stories will never be told. The saints who suffered were not all leaders and their names never hit the headlines. They belong to the great army of God's anonymous heroes. Through the long dark night they never wavered in their loyalty to Christ. For some of them the only release they ever knew was to be with Christ through death.

The darkest phase of all was undoubtedly the Cultural Revolution. The most intensive phase of this revolution, when the young Red Guards were in control, was 1966-69, but in fact the process lasted for ten years, presided over by the "Gang of Four." Of course the main target of the young revolutionaries was not Christianity, or even religion in general, but "revisionism." Mao wanted to ensure that a new policy of liberalization would not replace the fervent revolutionary spirit that had characterized the People's Republic. Anything that savored of the old order or the old culture was suspect.

The temples and holy places of Confucianism and Buddhism were destroyed, along with church buildings. Christianity, at least in its Western form, was virtually wiped out. Even the churches of the Three-Self Patriotic Movement were forced to close down. A spiritual winter descended upon the land. In the midst of this revolution Jiang Qing, wife of Chairman Mao and the leader of the Gang of Four said, "Christianity in China has already been put into a museum. There are no more believers." It certainly seemed that that was the case. But in wintertime it seems that all life has taken a leave of absence, although in fact beneath the surface it is being sustained and nourished, waiting to break forth with the advent of spring.

How individual Christian families fared is graphically illustrated by this account of the Luke family, told by Paul Kauffman:

> The entire family was at home when the Red Guards barged in. Two sons had graduated from a university under Communist instructors. They could not accept the Christian faith of their godly parents. Because the father had received his college education in America, the entire family, including the sons, was blacklisted as undesirable by the Communists.
>
> Entering the house, the Red Guards wantonly destroyed almost everything in sight. They discovered the life-savings which the Lukes had carefully kept for their sons' inheritance, and pocketed it. Then they demanded all Bibles and Christian books. The parents surrendered two Bibles and two copies of the book many Chinese Christians most value next to the Bible: *Streams in the Desert*. The Red Guard leader threw the books at the elder Luke saying "Destroy these books," and with that they left.
>
> Repulsed and disgusted by what they had seen, the two sons apologized profusely to the parents. Mr. Luke responded by saying, "Boys, the money I had saved for your inheritance is gone, but I have something far greater to give you." To each son he gave a Bible and

a copy of *Streams in the Desert.*
Since then, both boys have accepted the Lord.[5]

The long dark night for the church in China—and it is by
no means over—was no accident. God was not putting His
people through a survival course to see whether they would
make it. His promise holds true: ". . . I will build my church,
and the gates of Hades will not overcome it."[6] He was not
only building His church but was using the long dark night
to prepare China for what may well prove to be the greatest
spiritual advance in the history of Christianity. Let us now
look at how He was doing it.

7

CLEARING THE GROUND

*Herod and Pontius Pilate met together
with the Gentiles and the people of
Israel in this city to conspire against
your holy servant Jesus . . . They did
what your power and will had decided
beforehand should happen.*

Acts 4:27-28

Jesus once described the progress of the kingdom of heaven
as "...like yeast that a woman took and mixed into a large
amount of flour until it worked all through the dough."[7] In
the economy of God there is a secret, powerful spreading of
the kingdom that is vividly illustrated by what was taking
place in China's "long, dark night." When at length controls
were eased and restrictions lifted, Christians from outside
peered anxiously through the Bamboo Curtain to see if
anything had survived. They were astounded by what
began to emerge out of the dust and rubble of the Cultural
Revolution. There was no question as to whether the
Christian faith had survived. It was alive and well and
bursting forth with new growth on every hand.

During those dark years God had not been engaged in a
mere holding operation, waiting until better days to advance
the church. He was quietly but powerfully at work, purifying
His people and clearing the ground for a new planting that
He Himself would accomplish. China was no virgin soil
waiting for the first tilling and sowing. More than a hundred
years of missionary activity had gone before, and the
situation was not without mixture and confusion. God used
the Communist Revolution to perform a kind of clearing
operation. This is always how God likes to work. "I appoint

you over nations and kingdoms," He told Jeremiah, "to
uproot and tear down, to destroy and overthrow. . ." It
sounds like a divine mandate for a cultural revolution! Then
He added, "to build and to plant."[8]

It was God's intention to chalk up some important
lessons on the Chinese blackboard for His worldwide church
to ponder, but let us note first of all how He wiped the
blackboard clean. First, the Communist takeover meant the
removal of every missionary from China. God did not permit
the removal of the missionaries because they had failed in
their task. As we have already said, but for their past sowing
there would be no present reaping. They had accomplished
their task in the purpose of God, but it was now needful that
they move on to other spheres. In this way the next phase of
God's work in China could be accomplished.

We see the same principle at work in Paul, the pioneer
missionary. The New Testament missionaries never
established mission stations because they were never
stationary. But they did establish churches. Then often
persecution drove them out and drove them on, when, as we
would think, those churches were barely established.

In this the apostles were victims neither of the malice of
the devil nor of those who opposed them. Their steps were
being ordered by the Head of the church, who saw that their
exodus was essential for the growth of the young believers.
The moving on of the apostles facilitated the birth of new
young leadership.

There are many examples of the operation of this
principle in the history of the church. In 1935 Mussolini
invaded Ethiopia, and Protestant missionaries were
evacuated. When they returned six years later they
wondered if they would find anything left of their labors.
They found that the churches they had planted had not only
survived but had grown by leaps and bounds.

In China, God also used the Communists to sweep away
Western denominational structures. The Communists' case
against them was not so much that they were
denominational as that they were Western, and were, in
their view, the infamous tools of imperialism. The Catholic
church with its subservience to Rome has been replaced by

the Catholic Patriotic Association, headed by Marxists and totally independent of the Vatican.   It is the Catholic equivalent of the Protestant Three-Self movement.

It would be going too far to say that there is no denominationalism in China. The trappings can still be found in the open, or official, churches as well as in the attitudes and practices of some of the house churches, but the old structures have gone, and in great measure the deck has been cleared.

Out of the mixture that was the Christianity of pre-Communist China, God is surely preserving all that was truly the work of the Spirit. The gold, the silver, and the precious stones are finding their place in the new building that He is erecting, but much of the wood, hay, and stubble has been burned up in the Marxist conflagration. Like the three Hebrews in Nebuchadnezzar's fiery furnace, the only thing the churches have lost is their fetters, and in the flames they are finding God.

The purging work was not simply corporate, affecting the church; it was inevitably individual and personal as well. The Communist takeover put every professed disciple of Christ into the crucible. No one could have imagined how hot the flames would be, or how long the ordeal. The Lord was sitting, according to His Word, "as a refiner and purifier of silver." Every believer would be tested as to the reality of his faith. The spurious would be skimmed from the molten mixture. "Rice Christians" would quickly disappear from the scene. Materially they had nothing to gain but an awful lot to lose by a profession of faith.   Under such circumstances, who would want to be a nominal Christian?

Even among those who were genuine believers, there were searchings of heart and testings of motives. They professed to love the Lord, but how much was there of pure devotion to Christ?   God had given no promise that faithfulness to Christ would mean miraculous deliverance from persecution or even imprisonment. Had it been so, who could be sure that his motives were pure? "Those who are wise will instruct many, though for a time they will fall by the sword or be burned or captured or plundered."[9] Even among the true believers not all would come through the fire

unscathed. "Some of the wise will stumble, so that they may
be refined, purified and made spotless until the time of the
end."[10]

In the Cultural Revolution the young Red Guards made
bonfires of everything that was considered a "holy object."
The saints had to learn, as they saw Bibles, hymn books, and
other Christian literature going up in flames, that even such
things as these do not constitute the kingdom of God. The
loss, painful though it might be, would not rob them of their
fellowship with Christ.

The Christian life is not even dependent upon the
possession of a Bible, however beneficial and desirable that
may be. It is dependent on the indwelling Spirit. How
vulnerable the saints would have been through the centuries
had it been otherwise. Those first Christians of New
Testament times did not possess Bibles—a complete Bible
did not even exist until the close of the first century. Besides,
many of the early Christians were illiterate, and could not
have benefited even had they possessed a portion of the
Scriptures.

Geoffrey Bull was a missionary captured by the Chinese
Communists when they took possession of Tibet. During his
three years' incarceration they took his Bible from him. In
his book, *When Iron Gates Yield*, he records how God
sustained him, though he deeply regretted that he had not
committed more Scripture to memory. Persecuted saints
through the centuries have ever proved the grace of God,
even when cut off from the Bible, Christian books, and the
fellowship of other believers. We must all be behind every
effort made to supply Bibles to China. But this should not
obscure the fact that God is demonstrating in that land the
church's ability to expand with remarkable rapidity, as in
apostolic times, despite the absence or shortage of Bibles.

There was also a work of preparation being effected
throughout Chinese society. Communism has without
doubt done a great deal for China, even from the Christian
point of view. The unification of the script into modern
standard Chinese will greatly facilitate the rapid
evangelization of the nation, as the common language of
Greek did in New Testament times. Communism has

delivered the Chinese from their innate resistance to change, from crippling traditions, and has largely delivered the nation—at least the younger generation—from the harmful influences of Buddhism and ancestor worship.[11]

Another great achievement of the Communists has been in the building of roads and the supply of transportation and communications. This may be compared to the Romans building their roads through the Empire, which prepared the way for the spread of the gospel in the first century. So in China the evangelist may now convey his message from place to place in a way that was impossible in pre-Communist China.

Those "mountains" that stood in the way of the early missionary effort have in great measure been removed. Now the Communists are learning that success in destroying is one thing; ability to replace with something better is another matter. Communism has promised far more than it is able to deliver.

The Cultural Revolution was a self-inflicted wound that has left a deep scar on the life of the nation. The people worshiped Mao as God; now he lies like Dagon, flat on his face before the ark, without head or hands. Within the party there was bitter infighting. The heroes of yesterday have become the villains of today, and the people are left bewildered and insecure. As a result of the Cultural Revolution many urban workers lost their opportunity to better themselves through higher education, a grievous loss to most Chinese. It has left them depressed and disillusioned.

Why was President Liu Shaoqi, the man Mao had designated as his successor, toppled from power in the Cultural Revolution, disgraced and thrown into prison as "a lackey of imperialism"? Why, after Mao's death, was he posthumously "rehabilitated," as the Chinese call it, and his memory honored? These inexplicable swings of the political pendulum have left the average Chinese totally bewildered. Not many are sure what the current line is, and no one knows when it will change.

Fox Butterfield, one-time correspondent of the New York Times in Beijing, tells the story of a young Chinese woman called Bing. Her father was a general in the People's Liberation Army who had been unjustly singled out in the Cultural Revolution and accused of being a capitalist and a traitor. Bing herself, at that time a thirteen-year-old revolutionary, had been persuaded to testify against her father. He was sentenced to a military detention center. After ten years in prison he was "rehabilitated" and reconciled to his daughter. But the whole experience shattered Bing's faith in Marxism. She recounts:

> During the Cultural Revolution every household had a white plaster cast of Mao, and each day all the family members had to bow before it twice. The saying was, "In the morning ask for instructions; in the evening report back what you have done." For those of us who survived, the Cultural Revolution was a good thing. We learned a lot. I could never put another god in my heart like Mao.[12]

For Bing, the revolutionary spirit that once possessed her had been killed stone dead; in its place, a vacuum.

Someone has summarized the post-Mao situation in these words: "The hearts of one billion Chinese are searching for something to satisfy"—the "something" that communism cannot provide. This is one reason why millions are responding to the good news about Jesus.

Anyone visiting China from the West and inquiring about the Christian church will be assured by the authorities that there is religious liberty, and will be taken, if he so desires, to one of the open churches of the Three-Self movement to prove it. The official church leaders claim to speak for one united church of China. Independent house churches supposedly do not exist. What is the truth?

8

WHICH IS THE REAL CHURCH?

The mature . . . have their faculties
trained by practice to distinguish good
from evil.

Hebrews 5:14 (RSV)

It is difficult for Christians reared in democratic freedom to
understand the attitude of a totalitarian regime toward
religion. We make a clear distinction between politics and
religion. To the Communist there is no difference. His
concept of "government" is total control with no opposition.
"Your religion," he would tell the Christian, "determines
your way of life, your priorities, how you spend your spare
time and your money, and your attitude to government.
Your religion challenges the supremacy of the state. Of
course it's political."

In the same way, Communists view their ideology as if it
were religion, atheistic though it may be. Take the worship
of Chairman Mao, and the political "conversion" of
dissidents, involving confession of their political guilt and
indoctrination. Leading Chinese newspapers now refer to
widespread disillusionment concerning Marxism as "a
crisis of faith." Alexander Solzhenitsyn sums it up perfectly:
"Where the State is sovereign, there can be no place for any
other religion."

What the Bible has to say about this is very clear.
Governing authorities have been established by God, but are
therefore accountable to that higher and heavenly
authority. Only God has absolute authority. "Give   to

Caesar what is Caesar's, and to God what is God's."[13] When
Caesar demands what belongs to God alone, he has
overstepped his heavenly mandate and is acting without
divine authority. This is the key issue now facing the church
in China.

We have noted earlier how the Communists, within a few
years of gaining power, tried to unite all the churches under
a central umbrella—the Three-Self Patriotic Movement—
and made that body in turn subject to Party policy. Many
Christian leaders, like Wang Mingdao and Watchman Nee,
saw through this ploy from the start, and refused to
cooperate. To give to the state the allegiance that belonged
to the Lord alone was to them a betrayal of Christ. They
were not willing to do that, though it cost them dearly to
make this stand.

Tragically, it was often—and still is—Three-Self leaders
and members who played a leading role in the arrest,
accusation, and sentencing of Christians, whose only crime
was their refusal to give Caesar what belonged to Christ.
The attempt of the Communists to force the various
branches of the professing church to become one simply
insured that they would always be two: the open churches,
subservient to the Party, and the unofficial churches that
insisted, "We must obey God rather than man."

Many Christians' distrust of Communist intentions was
more than vindicated when the Cultural Revolution
overtook the nation. Even the official churches closed, and
every visible practice of Christianity ceased. We have seen,
however, that God was in control and was working
wonderfully to set the stage for a massive surge forward.

When restrictions were eased it became clear that the
underground church had had an underground explosion. As
mentioned earlier, before the Cultural Revolution there were
about one million Protestants and three million Catholics in
China. After the revolution reports came in of new believers
being numbered, not in thousands or even hundreds of
thousands, but in millions. The vast majority of these were
in the house churches. This growth has stirred up increasing
opposition from Three-Self leaders who have been more
active than ever in seeking to coerce the house church

leaders to join the Three-Self organization.   Where they would not cooperate, churches have been forcibly closed, and leaders arrested and interrogated.

When Three-Self representatives travel overseas they are at pains to stress that there is complete unity in the church in China and that they are the rightful representatives and spokesmen of that church. In the West the World Council of Churches seems to have swallowed their propaganda. We must realize that leaders of the house churches have no access to the media, and when the official church leaders insist that they do not want Bibles and other help from the West, they are not speaking for the silent majority of Christians in China who belong to the unofficial churches.

The Three-Self movement is now directing its attention to the evangelical churches, which are often in a quandary concerning what they hear about the church in China. Can they trust the statements of Three-Self leaders? Are these leaders truly following Christ? Why do so many Christians in China view them with distrust and refuse to join them? When Christian leaders visit China they are taken to packed Three-Self churches where sound evangelical sermons are often preached, good Bible correspondence courses are available, and Bibles are plentiful. Is the "official church"— its leaders hate being called this—the "real church"?

The conclusion we have to reach about the Three-Self Patriotic Movement is that it is good only in parts. Let us look at its three parts.

The worshipers who are undoubtedly thronging these "open" churches are mostly simple Bible-believing Christians, wanting baptism, the Lord's Supper, Bible teaching, and the warmth of fellowship with other Christians, most of which are things which have been denied them over the past years. The fact that the Three-Self church is controlled by the government doesn't really concern them.   Few have any real understanding of the spiritual and political implications.

The pastors and teachers, as in the churches of the West, are a mixture. Many have been recalled from factories and communes to shepherd the flock. Some are, or have since become, committed Christians who preach God's Word faithfully. Others are theologically liberal or are nominal Christians, and among these there are some who are rightly labelled "Judases." They have denied the faith during the Cultural Revolution, and now that the situation has eased, they have climbed back onto the bandwagon. In the leadership team of an open church, one man will be a political agent, responsible to see that Party rules are kept. The born-again pastors either ignore or turn a blind eye to the political implications of belonging to the Three-Self organization. They do not feel that politics is their concern. They are seizing the opportunity to preach the gospel and shepherd the flock. They say, "Three-Self is a good pond to fish in, so let's fish."

The "top brass," it would not be unfair to say, are politicians rather than spiritual leaders. Often they have proved themselves more "leftist" than Party officials, although this may be changing. As far as theology is concerned they are mainly liberals.

Their attitude to any evangelism may be summarized in one word: "Don't!" The history of the first thirty years of the Three-Self movement would suggest that there is little truth or spiritual reality in the top echelon. It is reported that at the thirtieth anniversary of the movement, they prayed for the aged pastor, Wang Mingdao. Who were they trying to impress? Why did they not rather repent of their shameless betrayal that put this faithful servant of God and his wife behind prison bars and robbed him of twenty-four years of public ministry? Time and again they have taken part in accusation campaigns against Christian leaders and collaborated with the authorities in having them removed from the scene.

The Three-Self movement has been likened to a pyramid. The higher you get in the movement the closer the links with the Party, and the more political you have to be. In reaching a conclusion about the official churches we must not allow our minds to be confused by the fact that there are very many truly born-again Christians in its ranks, nor that there are some devoted servants of Christ faithfully proclaiming God's Word in its pulpits. We have even heard of one minister who uses his position to warn the house churches of any measures to be taken against them. The fact remains that the top leadership of the movement is wrong. It is political, not spiritual. It is Caesar, not Christ.

The Three-Self movement is now the main agent of the Religious Affairs Bureau in attempting to suppress the burgeoning house church movement. Of course they would say they are not suppressing it but seeking to bring it under control. It amounts to much the same thing. Ding Guangxum, who heads up the Three-Self movement, confidently asserted in 1980 that there was no division between the Three-Self churches and the house churches. This is what he would like the world to believe. Having spoken to a Chinese brother who is regularly in touch with house church leaders all across China, I know that Ding's statement is far removed from the facts of the case.

The official churches have their "worship halls," buildings reopened for church services by permission of the Religious Affairs Bureau. These are the official "open churches." Then they have meeting points, which are house meetings located near the open churches, operating under Three-Self surveillance but having a measure of independence. The official church also has registered "home meetings" which came into being after 1958, when churches were closed. Though these groups are free to appoint their own preachers and to manage their own finances, their leaders must attend the Three-Self movement indoctrination classes to learn about Party politics.

All these are to be distinguished from the "free meetings" of the independent house churches, which have experienced such a phenomenal increase. These groups find the restrictions imposed by the Three-Self movement wholly unacceptable. Take, as an example, these "Ten Commandments" put out early in the eighties by the Three-Self movement in Henan Province.

1. Do not organize a church without the government's approval.
2. Except for government-appointed clergy, nobody should baptize.
3. Do not have contacts with foreign religious bodies or buy books from abroad. Violators will be prosecuted.

4. Do not print or reproduce Bibles and other religious books without approval.

5. Do not travel from commune to commune to spread religion.

6. Keep religion to yourself.

7. Do not pray every day. Pray only on Sundays.

8. Do not convey religious thoughts to persons under eighteen years of age.

9. Do not sing (religious) songs to youths under eighteen years of age.

10. Do not solicit contributions for promotion of religion, increasing believers' burdens.

Some of these injunctions may have been modified or even rescinded. But that certainly does not apply to the prohibition on influencing youth. Remember, the vast majority of those in the house church movement are young people. You may be sure that a body willing to impose such restrictions on the churches in the first place would be ready to reimpose them at any time should Party policy so dictate.

The latest measure to try to control the unofficial house churches is called the "three designates." It insists first that meetings may only be held in designated buildings; then, that only designated preachers may preach at meetings or visit private homes; and finally, that such preachers may not travel outside their own designated areas without a special permit. The designating authority in each case is the Religious Affairs Bureau.

Perhaps we are seeing in China the foreshadowing of what will be the case throughout the world before the end comes—a true church and a false church, each distinguished by its heart attitude to the lordship of Christ. The book of Revelation shows us these two in their final expression: the bride, "beautifully dressed for her husband," and the harlot, "drunk with the blood of the saints, the blood of those who bore testimony to Jesus."[14] Because there will be many of God's true children caught up with the harlot, just as there are in the Three-Self movement in China, a voice will sound from heaven before judgment falls: "Come out of her, my people, so that you will not share in her sins, so that you will not receive any of her plagues."[15]

Looking at these two expressions of the church there is no need to call out, "Let the real church in China please stand up!" It is standing up and being counted, at considerable cost.

9

MEET THE HOUSE CHURCH

Greet Priscilla and Aquila, my fellow
workers in Christ Jesus. They risked
their lives for me. Not only I but all the
churches of the Gentiles are grateful to
them. Greet also the church that meets
at their house.

Romans 16:3-4

We dismissed the taxi and made our way down a very long narrow street, almost like an alleyway. Fortunately there was no street lighting. The terraced shops and apartments provided just enough light to pick our way until we came to an unmarked doorway. A narrow flight of wooden stairs brought us to the second floor of the building. The stairs housed the overflow of the meeting which was in progress. Here were Chinese Christians, Bibles in hand and notebooks at the ready, listening to a voice coming over the loudspeaker. Up another flight of stairs, to a floor jammed with people of all classes. There were professional people and students mingling with working class people in their overalls, all sitting on simple wooden benches.

We were conducted to the only empty seats we could see. They had probably been reserved for us, since the leaders knew we were coming. We found ourselves within a few feet of the preacher, whose message was being relayed throughout the house. I had read of house churches in China that have 200 or more people and had often questioned how you could fit that number into a private home. Here I was, right in one. I counted over 150 people on that floor alone and even then could not see those tucked away in little rooms and cubbyholes.

This house church had four regular meetings each week: one for worship, one for prayer, one for sharing, and the mid-week Bible study, which we were attending. The house church leader who was speaking when we arrived, apart from a smile of welcome, seemed totally unaffected by our presence. The people also seemed far more preoccupied with the message than with the presence of the foreign visitors. There was a pause in the preaching, a song was announced, and the people began to sing to music relayed over the public-address system. Then the Bible teaching continued.

The house church leader, whom I would guess was about fifty, spoke the word with verve and authority. His face shone as he ministered, but it was not until afterward that I understood why. Our Chinese guide explained that he was a very courageous man of God who had spent many years in prison for his faith. He was highly respected by the other house church leaders in the area. On inquiring, we discovered that there were about 500 other house churches in this great city.

Because of the risk—not to the foreign visitors, but to their hosts—we stayed for only an hour, then slipped away into the dark of the street. I felt that I had for just those few minutes stepped into the pages of the New Testament.

The house church was a significant feature of New Testament Christianity. Believers also met in caves and catacombs, or in other places where much larger numbers could be accommodated. This is the situation with the house churches of China. Some, particularly in rural areas where the congregations may be quite large, have their own buildings; but most are, literally, churches in the house.

The church in China, like the church in New Testament times, is demonstrating that the possession of church buildings is not essential for rapid growth. So often the attitude of Westerners is that if you don't have a proper church building, you don't have a proper church. But it was not until the third century after Christ that Christians were permitted to possess church buildings.

House churches in China are not a recent development. They became a distinctive feature of Chinese Christianity during the early years of Communist rule. They did not come out of a reform movement that rejected traditional buildings in favor of a return to New Testament simplicity. No promoter of house churches traveled the country to spread the vision. Rather, the house churches came out of pressure and persecution. They were born from necessity. It was the best, and in most cases the only, way to meet. However, behind the outward circumstances was the strategy of the Holy Spirit, providing the setting for the tremendous growth that was to come.

If this simple structure that the Chinese believers adopted was thoroughly New Testament, it was also distinctively Chinese. We have already noted that a strong family bond is a national characteristic, and all the efforts of the Communists to destroy this have failed. When the pressures on the Christian family became great, it was natural that the home would become a place of refuge where family members could still worship, pray, read the Scriptures, and encourage one another.

Some China watchers see three phases of the house church movement. The first phase took place during the fifties as a direct result of Communist policy, and in particular because of the activities of the Three-Self movement against Christian leaders and their churches. Those who were unwilling to worship in the Three-Self churches had no alternative but to meet in their homes.

The second phase came with the Cultural Revolution in 1966, when even the Three-Self churches closed. Those who now wished to continue to worship God had no place but the home.

Then came the easing of restrictions in the post-Mao era, and with it an explosion of the house church movement. This was the beginning of phase three. It began before the reopening of the Three-Self churches, an important point since the Three-Self leaders like to claim that they are responsible for the resurgence of Christianity in China. When their churches did reopen, some who had left them when they closed down drifted back; but the vast majority did not, and have not joined the Three-Self organization.

Because of Communist policy in the fifties, it was impossible for denominational churches to survive in their original form. Either they came under the official church or they were forced to disband. At first the indigenous churches grew rapidly; then they had to go underground. Some of these did not survive, others joined the official church, while others again can still be identified among the house churches.

Many pastors who formerly led traditional churches have become involved in the house church movement. They find house churches more intimate, more "New Testament," and more Chinese in flavor than the Three-Self movement, with its political overtones and its formal Western-style services.

Not only are the Chinese family-oriented, they are also community-minded. There is no character in the Chinese language for "privacy." The idea seems foreign to their thinking. The absence of privacy hit me forcefully when I walked into a crowded restaurant in Shanghai. Everywhere there were round tables with eight or ten people, all eating from communal dishes as they talked excitedly to one another. Sharing is natural to the Chinese. This has had a profound effect upon the spread of the gospel, leading to not merely whole families but whole communities turning en masse to Christ.

Paul Kauffman tells of a family he knew in northern China. The two daughters, who were forced to stay in China when their parents left, found their faith dulled by Marxist teaching. However, the excesses of the Cultural Revolution brought them back to Christ. They both witnessed to their husbands and led them to Christ. The husbands won their parents. The parents in turn witnessed to other members of the family. Today, when the family meets for worship, there are at least nine adults present.[16]

According to a recent estimate, more than half of China's one billion people are under twenty. It is not surprising, then, that the house churches have a preponderance of people in their twenties and thirties. Some of them are ex-Red Guards. Others are simply victims of the political vacuum that came in the wake of the Cultural Revolution. They are disillusioned by the Party's swings of policy and by unfulfilled promises. Said a university student, "The structure of communism has crumbled in my mind, but I don't know what to do with the rubble." Others are embittered because they have been compelled to sacrifice higher education for the cause of the Revolution.

Suddenly these disillusioned young people find themselves confronted by a revolutionary spirit of another kind. They meet committed Christians who have been purified but not embittered by suffering, who have a joy and a holy optimism, and who witness without fear about another King and another kingdom. Thousands are finding this appeal irresistible, and whole communities are turning to Christ, Party officials and all.

Because 80 percent of Chinese live in rural areas, that is where most of the believers are to be found and where the greatest advances have been seen. Since the official churches and their influence are often confined to the cities, the rural house churches have been, to their great relief, less affected by Three-Self activity. Within the cities the policy is increasingly to try to close down the house churches and compel their members to attend a newly opened official church. The argument is that if you don't join the government-sanctioned Three-Self movement you are not patriotic; but most of the house church people, who are deeply loyal to their country, do not see that loving one's country means loving the Three-Self movement.

As in all indigenous movements of the Holy Spirit, these churches are strongly Bible-oriented. From the moment they are born into the kingdom, the young believers have a tremendous hunger for the Scriptures. This has not been dulled but rather sharpened by a shortage of Bibles. In many cases the sole owner of a Bible in a group will tear out pages, which are passed around—the community spirit again—and then laboriously copied by hand. Reports of only one Bible among hundreds of believers are not uncommon in the rural areas. Like most Orientals, the Chinese have prodigious memories. Lengthy passages, even whole books, are memorized. I heard of one Christian who learned the whole New Testament by heart.

Some of the larger house churches, like the one my group visited, are led by elderly pastors who have been released after spending twenty years or more in prison. These stalwarts of the faith who have come through the flames have done a great deal in teaching new Christians and in shepherding the flock.

The churches by and large are not pastor-dominated, and do not tend to be sermon-oriented. Without realizing it they have made a practical rediscovery of the "priesthood of all believers." In most cases, the leader, will give a brief message from the Bible, and then those present will share what they have found in the passage. In some groups everyone will have copied out the relevant passage the previous week, and will come to the meeting with his or her prepared thought.

In pre-Communist times, Christian women who went out preaching and evangelizing in the villages did a tremendous work, especially among the women folk. Some of these women are still to be found leading house churches, especially where pastors have been imprisoned or men are not available to lead the flock. They have played a significant part in the prospering of the work. I will say more about this later.

In country districts where Christians predominate, the churches are large and may be visited from time to time by traveling preachers. The service they perform involves outstanding courage and dedication. Beatings and imprisonment are the likely punishment should they be caught.

In a mountainous region of one of the coastal provinces there is a village with a population of 10,000. One-third of the inhabitants are believers. They began to worship openly in 1976, and now there are fifteen meeting places with an average of 200 attending in each place. Services are usually in the evening, from seven until eleven o'clock; they consist of singing, testimony, prayerful supplication, and Bible teaching from one of ten or more preachers who travel from meeting to meeting. Their messages usually last for an hour or more.

This group illustrates another important feature of Chinese Christians: they have a spirit of prayer, and they know how to exercise it. The Chinese have a saying, "Much prayer—much power!   Little prayer—little power!   No prayer—no power!" Some rise at 4:00 A.M. every day to pray for their country. People who have met with them speak of the spirit of urgency that characterizes their praying.

All over China, healing, deliverance from demonism, and other supernatural manifestations of the Holy Spirit's power are commonly experienced. It seems that these phenomena often flow from fervent prayer. Like the first Christians in Jerusalem, the Chinese have cried out to God to stretch forth His hand to heal, and to perform signs and wonders. Presently we will see how mightily God has answered those prayers, and what the impact has been upon the resultant harvest.

Besides the meetings in homes, in larger buildings, or in courtyards, and so on, there are the outdoor meetings. These are held in parks or cemeteries or in the countryside. Sometimes those attending meet as though having a picnic. They sing, pray, and witness. When they disperse, the church is not to be found until it meets again somewhere else. Early in the eighties this kind of meeting was common in Shanghai, but now all open-air meetings there have been banned. In the rural areas, where most of the Christians are, there are many meetings in believers' homes. As with the city house church described at the beginning of this chapter, the members put aside one night for prayer, another for Bible study, another for praise, and so on, and often meet all day Saturday and Sunday. Where there is interference by the Public Security Bureau the response is one of quiet resistance.   But often the house church members are so numerous that the authorities do not interfere.

The new converts are taught to evangelize others and are often in trouble for doing so. But instead of this hindering their faith it usually makes them stronger and more effective. The major work is being done by new converts who are still in their twenties. By the time they reach their thirties they are seen as being really experienced. "Children of the Cultural Revolution are very, very resourceful, experienced, and dynamic."[17]

The Christian leaders in these churches have developed instruction teams as well as evangelistic teams. In workers' training sessions the young Christians are taught to preach. When the leaders judge them fit they are commissioned and then they join the evangelistic team. In many of these villages the one desire in the hearts of believers is to preach and build churches. Their agricultural work is done simply to make a living, but most of their time is devoted to the Lord's work.

As these farming people seek first the kingdom of God, they find that "all these things"—the necessities of life—are added to them, just as Jesus promised. The Lord blesses their crops abundantly. When others' crops suffer from the drought, theirs thrive; when others' crops are spoiled by heavy rain, they have sunshine!

Evangelism is done in the evenings or during the off-season. Since 1982 the government has given back to individual house-owners much of the land that had been farmed by communes. As long as it is properly farmed, they are free to do other things. Wives and children help in the tilling of the land to enable their men to go out preaching. At harvest-time they will help each other, and then get back to their evangelistic work.

We have seen something of the characteristics and composition of these unofficial churches. Let us now look at their startling growth and then at some of the factors that make the house church movement in China the most rapid expansion of Christianity in our day, possibly the most rapid in the 2,000 years of the church's history.

10

THE SPREADING FLAME

*Oh, that you would rend the heavens
and come down, that the mountains
would tremble before you! As when fire
sets twigs ablaze and causes water to
boil, come down to make your name
known to your enemies and cause the
nations to quake before you!*

Isaiah 64:1-2

As the dust and rubble began to clear in post-Mao China it
was tremendously heartening to hear that behind the
Bamboo Curtain the church of Christ was alive and well,
and indeed, flourishing and growing. With the easing of
restrictions toward the close of the seventies, Chinese
Christians in Hong Kong and elsewhere were able to return
to China and visit families that they had not seen for many
years. It was then that the outside world began to see the full
extent of what God had been doing. There was talk of
"millions turning to Christ," of whole communities
becoming Christian. Understandably this was greeted with
incredulity in many quarters: "That can't be true—not in
Communist China!"

In a land so vast, where there were still such tight
restrictions, how could anyone be sure of these figures? Were
they wild guesses, or merely spiritual optimism? Was it like
some exaggerated reports often heard in the past of "crusade
conversions"? Certainly something wonderful was
happening, but what was the real extent of it?

Then more detailed reports came in from organizations
whose business it was to make a careful study of the Chinese
situation, and whose workers were regularly traveling to
and from the mainland. They also had opportunity to

question carefully those who had come out of China to Hong Kong. The reports began to be confirmed by many witnesses.

Now we have firsthand accounts of the sweep of this great movement of the Holy Spirit. The reports are not confined to select areas or to local "bright spots," although there are vast areas still untouched. The story has been the same, from the far north, where God is at work among banished Chinese in Mongolia, to the minority tribes that dwell among the mountains of the southwest; from the heavily populated coastal region, with its great cities like Beijing, Shanghai, and Guangzhou (Canton), to the plains made fertile by the great Yellow River. House churches are known to exist in almost all of the twenty-nine provinces, with their 2,000 counties.

Despite its history of wars and political upheavals China has seen the phenomenon of recurring revivals. This has been the case especially since 1930. And even since the Revolution there have been numerous localized revivals. It is necessary at this point to distinguish between successful evangelism, which is the ongoing responsibility of the church, and revival, which is a thing of special times and seasons. With evangelism, the work, however anointed, is necessarily man-centered. With revival, there is a spontaneity that tells us God has taken the field. By this definition, not all that is happening in China can be called revival. Much of it is the fruit of evangelism and zealous witnessing on the part of the church. But the way God has moved in some areas bears the unmistakable stamp of revival.

Asian Outreach, describing what was happening in China, said:

> There was unquestionably a gracious moving of the Holy Spirit that swept millions into the kingdom of God. Soon the church, purified by the fires of persecution and open to the miracle-working power of God, had to cope with what has been described as "the most rapid church growth in the history of Christianity." Never before, anywhere in the world, have so many accepted Christ in such a short period of time. This was not the result of a

planned evangelism program, but rather a spontaneous
move of God.

Time and again a fire from heaven has ignited the
prepared twigs, and the wind of the Spirit has fanned the
flames, sweeping them from place to place. This is how
many of the Christian leaders in China see it. A seventy-
year-old pastor, who one Sunday had preached to 500 people
in the morning and 1,000 in the evening, said, "The fire of the
gospel has been lit and it is going to keep on burning like a
prairie fire."

Let us first of all see how God is working in the distant
regions of China. Over the years many in disfavor with the
government, such as intellectuals, land-owners, and
Christians, were sent to labor camps in Mongolia. This
desolate province in the far north is the "Siberia" of China.
To be sent to a labor camp there is like a death sentence.
Many never return. In this bleak and inhospitable region
God has been quietly but powerfully at work, as the
following story reveals.

In 1980 an elderly Christian lady, one of a family of
intellectuals who previously had been banished to Inner
Mongolia, was constrained by the Holy Spirit to travel by
train thousands of miles south to Guangzhou (Canton). She
knew no one there, but was convinced that God would bring
her into contact with Christians. She providentially met
David Wang of Asian Outreach in the foyer of a hotel in that
city, and told him how the church was mushrooming in
Mongolia, with people coming to Christ in the most unlikely
places and in the most unusual ways. Out of the ministry of
the lady and her two sisters there are now 1,200 believers
meeting in forty house churches in that desolate land.

Inner Mongolia has a population of over nineteen
million, only two and a half million of whom are indigenous
Mongolians. Most of the remainder are Chinese. It is among
this latter group that God has been working. Now this group
in turn is reaching out to the Mongolians, who are staunch
Buddhists.

Moving from the far north to southwestern China, there
are minority tribes, the Miao and Lisu, who are similarly
responsive to the gospel. Of the 500,000 in Yunnan Province

it is estimated that 50 percent are Christians. Among the Lisu over the border in northern Burma the proportion is even higher—90,000 out of 120,000, or 75 percent. In some places entire Miao and Lisu villages have turned to Christ, and the Chinese authorities now view Christianity as the official religion of these two tribes. Often thousands of believers will gather on a mountainside to worship the Lord. As one eyewitness puts it, "Their singing ascends to the sky and hangs there like a cloud of glory." They pray and believe with the simplicity of little children, and the Lord often honors their faith with demonstrations of signs and wonders.

Now for the provinces nearer the eastern seaboard. Open Doors recounts how a Western Christian on a train met a young man who proved to be a Christian. To preserve his anonymity let's call him Tianying. He possessed a Bible that had been delivered to China by Open Doors. He had been led to Christ the previous year by his uncle, who had spent seven years in prison during the Cultural Revolution. Tianying, in turn, led his young wife to Christ in their home city in Henan Province. He said that the population of his city was about 300,000, and he believed that 100,000 professed to be Christian. Of the 6,000 in his commune, 2,000 were believers. Most of these were in their twenties and had come to Christ in the last two or three years.

His fellowship group of thirty believers met for two or three hours every Sunday night. Sometimes there was not one Bible among them. Hymnals and other Christian books were even more scarce. The meetings, he told the Westerner, consisted of singing, testimonies, prayer, thanksgiving to God, and Bible reading (when a Bible was available). Occasionally an itinerant preacher would visit their fellowship to teach the Word of God.

Courageous witnessing is by no means the prerogative of the grown-ups. Here is the testimony of a fifteen-year-old boy—let's call him Chiang—from Fujien Province, telling of his experience during the Cultural Revolution when he was only a teenager. A Christian sister from his house church, while she was in the hospital, was able to share the gospel with the woman in the next bed, who had been a fervent idol

worshiper all her life. Later, on this woman's discharge from
the hospital, Christians in the house church led her and her
daughter to the Lord.

The one big fear of the mother was her husband. He was a
huge and violent man, and a staunch Communist
cadre.[18] He was due to come home shortly from the country,
where he was in charge of a commune and labor camp. How
could she dare let him know that she had become a
Christian? As it was, every day he lost his temper and got
mad at her. This might be too much.

The Christians prayed fervently, and the Communist
cadre was invited to visit brother Chiang's family, as his
wife had told him how kind they had been to her in the
hospital. The Word of God was like a fire in Chiang's heart.
He knew he had to tell this man, who could well drag them all
off to prison, that they were Christians. Out came the truth.
The man, angry and red in the face, told the lad that this was
nothing but superstitious nonsense.   Amazingly, the
mixture of abuse and Marxist rhetoric did not extinguish the
fire of the boy's zeal. He found himself answering the big
man to his very face. God's Word was indeed a fire, and the
truths of creation, sin, and judgement were laid bare.

The hardened cadre was left dazed and speechless. As he
saw his sin and God's awesome holiness he began to
tremble. The impossible was happening. There, in Chiang's
humble Christian home, the visitor, with great tears of
repentance, found the Savior. His wife recently wrote to
Chiang, telling him that ever since that day her husband
had not once lost his temper, and that they daily read the
Bible, sang, and prayed together.[19]

A worker in Asian Outreach tells of what happened to a
Western missionary on a train journey in China. At a
scheduled stop a young peddler entered the compartment.
Trying to make conversation with the foreigner, he said in
his very broken English, "I am Christian. You Christian?"
With his fluent Mandarin, the missionary could have eased
things for this young man, but he coolly replied in English,
"Yes, I am a Christian."

Perhaps the young man had gleaned that most
Westerners like to think that they are Christian because they

belong to a so-called Christian country. Anyway, he wasn't satisfied, and pressed the point: "Are you a two-time born Christian?" Still the missionary held back and asked this young man to explain. He was turning red with excitement as he tried so hard to get this uninformed white fellow to understand what the new birth was all about.

At length the missionary took pity, and told him that he spoke Chinese. The young man's face shone, as he began to explain in his native tongue what it means to be a true Christian. The missionary was amazed both at his enthusiasm and his sense of urgency. "You must become two-time born Christian!" he urged. At length the missionary explained that he was both born again and a missionary.

"Good!" proclaimed the boy. "How many did you bring to Christ last month?"

The story did not reveal how the missionary responded to that "fast ball," but he discovered that this young man had been in training for the People's Liberation Army when he was converted and compelled to leave. Returning to his village, he joined a rapidly growing fellowship. When they saw that he had the gift of evangelism they helped him to get a license so that he could sell on the trains. "I love to tell everyone about Jesus," he said. "We must work while we have opportunity, because Jesus is coming back soon."

Proof of the manner in which this work of God is spreading is supplied when Christians from outside revisit a place and find that the tally of believers has multiplied incredibly. At the end of 1979 workers from Asian Outreach visited a village, part of a large commune, in Xinjiang Province. There were few Christians in that village, they were told. Six months later they returned and were told, "Now there are few unbelievers in the village!" Since then there has been a spiritual awakening in the whole area. The visitors were told, "This is now a Christian commune, and there are very many such in this province."

Paul Kauffman tells of his interview with a man of twenty-eight who came across to Hong Kong. As a schoolboy he had, like so many, rejected the faith of his parents and accepted the philosophy of Marxism. Through the witness of a friend, he yielded his life to Christ, was baptized, and became part of the house church. In his home city, with a population of 400,000, he reckoned there were 50,000 Christians. That works out to one in eight. Only one pastor had come through the Revolution. He was over eighty, but had an active ministry of Bible teaching and counseling.[20]

A remarkable feature of this movement is the way God uses the elderly who are now free after years in prison. Many are retired, so they are free to travel and don't need to earn their livelihood. They are the backbone of the leadership of the house churches. Aged pastors experience unbounded joy as they teach and preach again and see the response of the young people to their ministry. One ninety-year-old pastor returned to his village in southern China, and a church of 700 members sprang up there in just three months! Another similarly built a church of 400 members in western China.

The story of what God has done in a provincial capital of the east coast is amazing. By 1973 there was a Christian community of over 1,000. The authorities became alarmed and ordered the meetings to cease. The following year five leaders were arrested, paraded in dunce caps, and imprisoned. On release they continued their pastoral ministry, and the numbers of believers increased dramatically.

In this same city, a Chinese bishop whose predecessor had been tortured to death in 1980 reported that believers in the city numbered 2,000. Further afield, in seven remote mountain villages he had visited in the course of his pastoral ministry, he found 7,000 new Christians being taught by two elderly workers. By 1980 Christians throughout the province were known to number 600,000. In one area in a single year 6,000 new believers were baptized. Christians were beginning to appear even in Communist Party ranks and in the Youth League.

Still more remarkable is what God is doing in many of the communes. This report comes from the coastal province of Zhejiang: There is one commune of 10,000 which is totally Christian. The officials have named the production teams

"Jesus Team Number One, Jesus Team Number Two," and so on, and they have been held up as an example to other communes because of their consistently high production levels.

One could describe what is happening in many parts of China as "group conversion." It usually comes about when there is a powerful working of the Holy Spirit in a group or community. It begins with the conversion to Christ of a recognized leader or a number of leaders. This produces a chain reaction, and the group turns en masse to Christ. It is not a psychological phenomenon, or a case of the pack slavishly following the leader. Each one must respond personally. That is why some prefer the expression "multi-individual" conversion rather than "group conversion." It is just that God uses one decision to trigger off another.

The strong family ties and the strong sense of community among the Chinese make this a likely event, especially when the Spirit of God is moving powerfully. Of course this has worked both ways. It was those very family and community relationships in the pre-Revolution era that made the task of evangelism so difficult for the missionary.

The inland province of Henan has witnessed this incredible "people movement." With a population of seventy million, "astounding numbers have been turning to the Lord, whole villages or production teams at a time." In one county it is estimated that the Christians number 300,000 out of a population of 700,000. They are actively supporting and participating in witness teams who are spreading the gospel.

Leslie Lyall, an expert on China and a former missionary to that land, records, "In some rural areas over 90 percent of the population are Christian"—and this he describes as "a totally unprecedented statistic in the history of the church in China." It is probably unprecedented in the history of the church anywhere.

None have been used more in spreading the flame in China than the itinerant preachers. None have paid a heavier price in the fulfillment of their calling. Before we look at other means that God has been using, let us hear the challenging words of one preacher who has been "tramping for Jesus" since the sixties. Somehow he has avoided arrest, although many times he has had narrow escapes. He says:

> Although I give very little, the Lord receives my service. The Lord continues to train me and lead me in the revival work as He puts me among believers all over the land. Thank the Lord for His mercy.
>
> The Lord does not give us worry-filled hearts; rather our hearts are filled with peace and consolation. The Lord loves us, so what can people do to us? He whom we trust gives us strength so that we can do all this. Thank the Lord for His grace. We know we must obey our Lord, not men, because He gives us His precious power and faith. When we go preaching from village to village the Lord gives us these words to console us. We know that those who trust in Him will be rich and blessed. We praise and thank the Lord that now the powerful fire of His revival is spreading. The miracles of His power extend to all the lands. The faith in the hearts of the itinerant preachers brings that fire to all places, and then the fire spreads from one place to the next, from one province to another.[21]

This account could not be complete without special mention of the outstanding part that women have played in "spreading the flame." Back in the early missionary days many Chinese women trained in Christian schools and local churches dedicated their lives to Christ's service and became known as "Bible Women." In those days women in China were very secluded and did not attend public meetings. It was the Bible Women, along with the lady missionaries, who reached them in their homes—visiting the sick, teaching hygiene and child care, and befriending these "inside persons." Later, when such women began attending church, the Bible Women would teach them to read and write, for most were illiterate. These women were also involved in village evangelism.

During the first thirty years under the Communist regime when so many pastors, evangelists, and leaders were in prison, it was primarily the Bible Women, though no longer called by that name, who stepped into the breach and kept the churches together. Where a Barak is unwilling or not available for the task, God does not hesitate to raise up a Deborah. There are aged "Deborahs" still feeding flourishing churches in China, as in the case of the ninety-year-old woman who has a congregation of over 500 believers. Another wrote to Marjorie Baker, a former missionary to China, "I made a trip to the villages once every two months last year to preach the gospel. God worked in people's hearts and many were saved. A blind man and a mentally ill person were healed."

There is now a whole new generation of young people in the house churches who have grown up under Communism. The willingness of the young women among them to suffer for Christ has not been less than that of the young men. Hua Ling, as we will call her, is now twenty-one. She was born in a village in central China. At the age of eleven she came across a hand-copied booklet that told the way of salvation. In childlike faith she trusted in Christ. She never met another Christian, nor did she have a Bible, but she read and re-read the little booklet. How she longed to share the Good News with others. When some political relaxation came in 1980, she witnessed to her mother and some neighbors, and they were converted.

Hua Ling realized that God had given her the gift of evangelism. He continued to bless her ministry and brought her in touch with other Christians. They shared testimonies and worship, and built each other up. The message of the gospel spread. Many came to believe. Hua Ling, seeing the fields white for harvest, decided to become a full-time evangelist. Not fearing reproach, she gave up her job and went with others to spread the gospel in neighboring villages. Everywhere she went people turned to Christ. Revival came to the villages and Christians were renewed in their faith.

A retreat for people from eighteen to forty years old was organized at the time of the Spring Festival; 190 attended. The theme was "The Needs of the Harvest Field." Many present wept before the Lord and expressed willingness to give up their jobs and give themselves to evangelism. The leaders selected those they felt were called of God.

Hua Ling and her colleagues have experienced suffering and persecution in both the towns and the countryside. They have been beaten, kicked, and stunned by electric shocks.

Three of the brothers in their party were arrested and detained. Far from being frightened, they rejoiced to be counted worthy to suffer for Christ.[22]

God has also greatly used the radio in spreading the flame. It is said that all of China listens to the radio. China travelers report that they can pick up clear Christian broadcasts in even the farthest corners of the country. They continually meet those who testify to finding Christ through the radio broadcasts. Pastors and leaders eagerly devour the programs specially designed to help them in their ministry; countless Christians tune in regularly for spiritual food. A Christian leader in Hong Kong reported to me that the believers on the mainland tell him, "We don't want classical music (between programs). The time is too precious. Use it for preaching the gospel, or for feeding us Christians!"

It is almost impossible to comprehend a movement so vast in its scope and so rapid in its multiplication. Inevitably we begin to ask questions. What are the causes of this unprecedented move of God? Are there some "success secrets" here that we can learn and apply? It needs to be said at once that the ways of God can never be reduced to a spiritual formula; they are not as simple as that. In the first place there are always mystery elements—inexplicable factors bound up with the will and the timing of God. We have to remember that God always reserves the right to do "... as he pleases with the powers of heaven and the peoples of the earth,"[23] and He is under no obligation to "give an account of all His doings."[24]

Nevertheless there are vital lessons for us to learn. So before we enquire, "What can we do to help the church in China?", it may be more appropriate—and certainly more humbling—to ask the question, "What does the church in China have to teach us?" Without doubt God is writing many things on the China blackboard that He wants us to learn. We may find that not all the lessons are ones we are eager to embrace. As this book now moves from the "China story" to considering the spiritual lessons in it, let us ask God to give us humble, teachable, and willing hearts.

PART TWO

The Church in China Speaks

11

BLOOD RED SOIL

In truth, in very truth I tell you, a grain
of wheat remains a solitary grain unless
it falls into the ground and dies; but if it
dies, it bears a rich harvest.
John 12:24 (NEB)

Many years ago some tourists were visiting the Colosseum, Vespasian's famous amphitheater in Rome. "Take a handful of the soil," said the guide, "it's all martyrs'." I recall the sense of awe that came upon me when I too gazed on that great arena when visiting Rome as a soldier. This was the spot where Nero loosed the lions on Christians for the entertainment of the nobility of Rome. The martyrs' crime? They had confessed, "Christ, not Caesar, is Lord." Nero and the pomp of ancient Rome have passed away, but the kingdom for which those early Christians suffered and died marches on in triumph.

Those were the crude and cruel days of the first century, we may think, but hasn't our advancing civilization changed all that? May we not now accomplish the triumph of the kingdom without blood and tears? The words of Jesus at the head of this chapter may be familiar to us. We may see them fulfilled in the cross of Christ. Was He not that grain of wheat that fell into the ground and died? Are we not the harvest? True, but not the whole truth. We cannot bury the cross in history and assume that the "life out of death" principle that Jesus was talking about was totally fulfilled at Calvary. He Himself taught that every disciple must take up the cross and carry it with Him. The church in China will tell you that for them, the cross is very much a present experience, though worked out in a variety of ways.

Here, surely, is the primary reason why the work of the Holy Spirit in China is more swift, spontaneous, and powerful than anything we generally experience here in the West. These believers have a totally different attitude from Western Christians to suffering, hardship, and persecution . To us, these may be the unfortunate and occasional "accidents" of the Christian life, to be avoided if at all possible. When they do occur we probably view them as attacks of Satan to be resisted in the name of the Lord, and we trust for speedy deliverance. Let us test this attitude by the consistent teaching of the New Testament.

From the outset of His ministry Jesus warned His disciples to be ready for persecution. He did not wait until they were all fully mature and wholly sanctified before He introduced them to this "nasty" side of the Christian life. One reason for this is that persecution and suffering have a very real part to play in that same maturing and sanctifying process. In His first discipling course Jesus said, "Blessed are those who are persecuted because of righteousness," and He gave no hint that this "dubious blessing" would pass away as the gospel goes on to triumph in this age.

Jesus then went on to stress the importance of this beatitude by amplifying it in a way that He did not do with any of the others. He continued, "Blessed are you when people insult you, persecute you and falsely say all kinds of evil against you because of me. Rejoice and be glad, because great is your reward in heaven, for in the same way they persecuted the prophets who were before you."[25] That's heavy stuff for new converts!

When Jesus himself came to face the cross, He never faltered. "Now my heart is troubled," He confessed, "and what shall I say? 'Father, save me from this hour'? No, it was for this very reason I came to this hour. Father, glorify your name!"[26] Jesus never looked for a way out, He only looked for a way through—that He might glorify the Father in the path of suffering.

That little band of disciples was evidently not demoralized by what Jesus had said and by what He later experienced. Following Pentecost they began to witness, as Jesus had commanded them, in the power of the Holy Spirit. The opposition that Jesus had predicted was not long in coming. After being flogged and then ordered not to speak in the name of Jesus, "The apostles left the Sanhedrin, rejoicing because they had been counted worthy of suffering disgrace for the Name."[27]

Paul's initiation into the Christian faith was no different from that of his fellow apostles. From the time of his conversion on the road to Damascus the Lord began to "show [Paul] how much he must suffer"[28] for His sake. Paul in turn encouraged his new converts "to remain true to the faith," warning them, "We must go through many hardships to enter the kingdom of God."[29] A little later he wrote to the church in Philippi. He exhorted them to conduct themselves in a manner worthy of the gospel of Christ, and not to be frightened by the opposition. Then he informed them, "For it has been granted to you on behalf of Christ not only to believe on him, but also to suffer for him..."[30] Has anyone— besides Paul—ever told us that along with the privilege of believing in Christ, we have been accorded the privilege of suffering for Him?

Paul saw the dynamic of this principle as the secret of the incredible effectiveness and abiding fruitfulness of his own ministry and that of his fellow workers. He explained it this way:

> We have this treasure in jars of clay to show that this all-surpassing power is from God and not from us. We are hard pressed on every side, but not crushed; perplexed, but not in despair; persecuted, but not abandoned; struck down, but not destroyed. We always carry around in our body the death of Jesus, so that the life of Jesus may also be revealed in our body. For we who are alive are always being given over to death for Jesus' sake, so that His life may be revealed in our mortal body. So then, death is at work in us, but life is at work in you.[31]

Without any doubt the unparalleled harvest being reaped in China today is directly related to the way the church there has willingly embraced the way of the cross and continues to do so. "A grain of wheat," said Jesus, "remains a solitary

grain unless it falls into the ground and dies; but if it dies, it
bears a rich harvest." For China this is not a feature peculiar
to the late twentieth century. It has been true there since the
church was planted. Many indeed are the grains that have
fallen into the ground and died. See how great the harvest!
In the words of Samuel Zwemer,

> There is no grain without a loss,
> You cannot save without a cross.
> The corn of wheat to multiply
> Must fall into the ground and die.
> Whenever you ripe fields behold,
> Waving to God their sheaves of gold
> Be sure some corn of wheat has died,
> Some saintly soul was crucified,
> Someone has wrestled, wept and prayed,
> And fought hell's legions undismayed.

It began with the pioneer missionaries. It is easy for us,
living in the comfortable affluence of the twentieth century,
to be armchair critics of that early missionary movement.
Mistakes were made, and it would be foolish of us not to learn
from them. But when it comes to hardship, suffering, and
sacrifice, we have to sit at the pioneers' feet. Speaking of his
own pioneer evangelism, Paul once said, "I do not consider
my life of any account as dear to myself, in order that I may
finish my course, and the ministry which I received from the
Lord Jesus...."[32] Those pioneer missionaries to China may
not have understood much about apostolic ministry but they
certainly possessed the apostolic spirit.

The call to China meant a five month voyage, cooped up
in some cargo ship, before the missionaries even saw the
people to whom they had been called. Then they found
themselves "strangers in a strange land," coping with a
different climate, a different diet, a different culture, and
many months of strenuous grappling with a strange
language—all this before they could even make themselves
understood! Then for many there were the hardships of
pioneering the gospel among people who were initially
suspicious, prejudiced, and unresponsive.

There were no jets to whisk them away to the homeland
and give them a furlough every year or two. Some of them
never saw their homeland again. Outbreaks of violence like

the Boxer Rebellion took their toll. Young parents sometimes faced the agony of little ones struck down with fatal diseases, and then tearfully laid to rest in the soil of China. But for almost all, hardships, suffering, and self-denial were the order of the day. Like Paul, they knew what it was to die daily. "We always carry around in our body the death of Jesus . . . are always being given over to death for Jesus' sake." Day by day the price of the harvest was paid as seeds fell into the ground and died.

For some there was immediate reward, but many never saw a full harvest. If they were alive they would see it now. As a servant of God once said to me, "If you suffer without reaping, it is that others may reap after you. And if you reap without suffering, it is because others have suffered before you." Suffering and reaping are forever joined in God's plan.

Though we understand in the natural realm that the grain of wheat has to die before the harvest can come, we may wonder why this has to be true in the spiritual realm. In the first place, suffering is a means of purifying. It is like a threshing instrument. None of us likes being "threshed," but how else is the chaff in our lives to be separated from the grain? None of us relishes being subjected to the flame, but how else is the dross to be separated from the gold? A pure church is a powerful church, one through which the Spirit may flow unhindered.

There is a sense in which the cross comes to cleanse the church from racial and cultural impurities. This has happened in China, as Carl Lawrence has vividly expressed:

> Slowly, surely, we can hear the quiet procession of the shuffling feet, from every part of China, as they made their way to a hillside; there was the sound of someone digging, and then the thump of a cross being set upright; the pounding of nails, and slowly, old superstitions, ancestral worship, arrogance of being a superior race, bitterness for feeling they have been forgotten, ambitions, desires, security, creature comforts; the hills of China were alive with hundreds of years of history hanging from crosses. A twentieth century Nero helped purify Christ's church.[33]

Then, as we saw earlier in this book, God has used the Communist Revolution in great measure to purify "a fragmented denominational church which reflected all the idiosyncrasies of Western individualism," causing it to be a suitable instrument in the hands of the Holy Spirit.

> Hence the history of the church in China since 1949 has been a history of suffering. Yet by going through different stages of suffering, the church in China has been transformed from a timid, foreign-colored institutional church into a bold, indigenous institutionless church, and it has been changed from a dependent mission church to an independent missionary church. It is a church that has gone through the steps of the cross, following the footsteps of her Lord: betrayal, trial, humiliation, abandonment, suffering, death, burial, resurrection, and the gift of Pentecost . . . Christians in China interpret the last thirty-four years of prolonged suffering as a gift of God's profound grace to the Chinese church to cleanse her from her impurities, to test the genuineness of her faith and loyalty, to train her for obedience and progress unto greater maturity, and to enable her to gain a deeper experience of Christ.[34]

It has been said that "the Chinese church has from the beginning been a martyr church," but never a church with a martyr spirit. It is not eaten up with self-pity because of its hard lot, but is joyful and triumphant.

Again and again the consistent joy of believers has been the powerful magnet attracting fellow Chinese to a forbidden faith. Take this eyewitness account of believers being driven away to prison:

> The people of the street could not see the people inside the cart, but they thought that they were awful criminals to be dragged away like animals. The authorities did not want us to see them. "Are they really that sinful?" we asked. Then we found out the truth. These were Christians on their way to jail. They were all handcuffed together and they were happy. There was no dissatisfaction or resentment on their faces. We could hear them singing as they went by, "Lord, you are worthy to receive praise. Praise the Lord."

Or take this story of a sister who spent twenty-four years in prison:

She was in prayer when the authorities arrived to arrest her. She was not surprised, as the Lord had already prepared her heart. In fact, just as they arrested her, the Holy Spirit came and filled her with an uncontainable joy. As the car in which she was being taken away jostled down the road, she was overflowing with joy and sang all the way. The authorities naturally suspected that she was demented.

As she was being registered at the prison she had time to witness at length to one of the officials. So powerful was her anointed witness that right then and there he accepted Christ. As he registered her she said to him, "Today is not the day I came to register myself, and I will never really be a prisoner here—Christ will constantly be with me. I am free. This is the day when you have registered your residency in the kingdom of God."

Some time later, all the inmates were given an envelope containing the length of their sentence. The other inmates asked her how long her sentence was. She answered, "I don't know. I just put the edict away without looking at it."

"Why?" they asked. "Don't you want to know how many years you are getting?"

"It doesn't matter," she replied. "Whether it is ten years or one hundred years, each day will be a day with my Lord."

In one prison they were inhumanely crowded—ten prisoners to a tiny cubicle. They were not allowed to speak to each other or doze off during the day. A guard periodically looked into the room through a glass opening in the door. Many fell ill; others lost their minds. One prisoner whispered to her, "We can see that your religious faith really gives you strength."

Another day the guard burst into the room and shouted at her, "Stop your smiling."

"I am not smiling," she replied.

"Yes, you are," shouted the guard.

When he left, the other prisoners said, "Your eyes are always smiling and your face glows with joy, even when you are not smiling." Most of her fellow prisoners were not Christians—that is, they were not Christians until she led numbers of them to the Lord.

The word "martyr" is the Greek word for "witness." This suggests to us that from the earliest times a martyr church and a witnessing church were one and the same. That is certainly true in China, as this story told by David Wang reveals:

Martha was 18, young both in age and Christian experience, when I first met her in central China. She had become a Christian through listening to our radio broadcasts. She corresponded with us in Hong Kong and we nurtured her. Two years later I had the opportunity to meet this young Chinese girl again. She was working in a factory, but she urged us to let her do something for the Lord. She did not want money, or a bicycle. What she wanted was to be regularly supplied with Bibles, so that she could distribute them to the remotest provinces of China.

Martha was never on our payroll. But, from time to time, we helped to cover her traveling expenses. She was traveling and ministering, looking to God to meet her needs. I recall meeting her once in the city of Xian in 1981. We had arranged to meet at 9:00 p.m., but she did not turn up until about 1:00 a.m. She had been delivering Bibles in a nearby village when the local commune leaders discovered what she was doing. They beat her up, robbed her, and threw her onto a deserted road. It was only a miracle that she was able to hitchhike to our rendezvous.

Even in the darkness of the park, I noticed that something was wrong with Martha. Her head was swollen like a basketball.

"What is the matter with you?" I asked. "Did they beat you up like this?"

"Oh no," she said, "I've had this problem for nearly two months now." Then she rolled up her pants to show me legs covered with stings and mosquito bites. "I think it's some kind of blood poisoning." As she traveled in the remote countryside of China, often she had to sleep in deserted huts and derelict temples. She was being literally "beaten up" by bugs and mosquitoes.

"Tomorrow we must go to a doctor," I urged her.

"No, no," she said. "I have to catch an early train tomorrow to go to Inner Mongolia. Where are the Bibles?" Her only concern was to get the Bibles to Inner Mongolia.

Two years later, in August 1983, we suddenly lost contact with Martha. There was no news from her or about her for a long time. It was the time of China's "Anti-Crime Campaign." Many people were arrested and executed throughout China. We became quite concerned for Martha.

Later we got a letter from her through her friends. It was not really a letter, just a little piece of paper. She had been arrested and charged with distributing "superstitious materials" in the People's Republic of China. The little note read: "I don't know what the penalty will be, but please"—quoting Paul's words—"pray for me that whenever I open my mouth, words may be given me so that I will fearlessly make known the mystery of the gospel, for which I am an ambassador in chains." A few weeks later, we received news that 24-year-old Martha was "with Christ." She had been executed.

Yes, the soil of China has been made rich by the blood of its martyrs.

O cross, that liftest up my head,
I dare not ask to fly from thee,
I lay in dust life's glory dead,
And from the ground there blossoms red
Life that shall endless be.
George Matheson

12

BY THIS THEY CONQUER

*They have conquered him [Satan] by the
blood of the Lamb and by the word of
their testimony, for they loved not their
lives even unto death.*

Revelation 12:11 (RSV)

The progress of the kingdom in China is, in so many ways
strikingly similar to what we find in the New Testament. It
advances in the teeth of relentless opposition, and it is being
paid for with blood.

Paul tells us that the reception of the gospel by those in
Thessalonica was with "severe suffering" and yet with a joy
inspired by the Holy Spirit. From their conversion onward
these believers were aggressive in their witness for Christ.
Paul told them that they were a "model" to the churches
throughout Greece.[35] They are surely a model to the
churches of all time.

This is how it is in China. In the hearts of thousands of
Chinese believers, God has lit a flame that is a challenge and
a rebuke to the easy-going Christianity in the West. As in the
epic story of Elijah on Mount Carmel, the authorities have
poured their barrels of water on the sacrifice, and the fire of
God has come, not only consuming the sacrifice, but even
licking up the water in the trench.[36]

In their evangelism, the house churches of China do not
seem to put any stress on the diplomatic approach, or on
waiting for what we like to call "the God-given opportunity."
No doubt there is a place and time for this. But in China, God
is on the move, and the saints are moving with Him. As we

have seen, itinerant preachers go from village to village and county to county proclaiming the good news, often to quite large gatherings. Locally, the believers who have been trained in evangelism are organized into teams, and go forth to witness to all who will listen. They all know the penalties for breaking the rules—arrest and interrogation, beatings and imprisonment—but none of these things deter them.

A report late in 1983 spoke of the arrest of nineteen church leaders in one county in the north of China, and of eighty others who were forced to flee from their homes because of the threat of arrest. As the more seasoned pastors are arrested, or are forced to flee, a new generation of leaders is taking their place.

Younger men and women are also taking over some of the itineraries of the older preachers, who are now in prison or in self-imposed exile. In the face of restrictions, they travel circuits with many villages, preaching and counseling daily. They keep up exhausting schedules, often traveling fifty to sixty miles a day by foot, and ministering late into the night.

Christians see the hand of God even in this persecution, for those in prison are now able to sleep regularly for the first time in many months. Those who have fled their homes have gone into other provinces where they continue to spread the gospel.[37]

A group of house church leaders met in central China. Their major concern was the growing opposition of the Three-Self Patriotic Movement to any evangelistic outreach. They were determined to reach out for Christ in spite of it. Here is the gist of the seven-point resolution they adopted and circulated in their churches:

1. Let the message of the cross be spread wherever we go. We must make every believer know clearly that he is saved by the blood of the Lamb.

2. Our situation is a precarious one. We are under heavy pressure, and many brothers and sisters are being arrested by local authorities. Our meetings are being stormed and dispersed. Our Bibles are taken away, so we see clearly that we have to tread the path of the cross. We must have a willingness to suffer for Christ.

3. Many believers are still very confused as to the real

design of the Three-Self Patriotic Movement, and its power is getting stronger every day. In a way it is good to have the Three-Self open churches in the cities so that believers can have places for worship. But for us in the villages, the setting up of the Three-Self meeting points (also known as house churches) is a trap. Those who fall into that trap can no longer serve the Lord according to the leading of the Holy Spirit. The Three-Self movement forbids itinerant preachers to preach the gospel in places where it is most needed. They also forbid Christian workers from different places to have fellowship with each other; thus we can no longer hold larger meetings. But we are able to hold smaller meetings of eighty to a hundred people at night. We have to meet in different homes each night, just as we used to before 1976. But God is blessing house church meetings, and is opening wide for us doors which no one can close.

4. We are to build the church on the foundation of Jesus Christ. We are called to be builders of His church. So we must teach the people what the church of Christ really is. All our work must be arranged according to the biblical teachings of the church, and we must make Christ the center of our life's work.

5. We are stepping up fellowship among Christian workers so that we are linked together in love, and together we will work towards a general goal of evangelism of China.

6. To strengthen the church we must have the life of Christ to supply that life to other new members. We must train more young workers so that they can shepherd the new converts and let them grow in their life in Christ.

7. This is the idea of preaching the gospel as we tread the land, claiming the land for Christ's kingdom. Wherever we go, we preach Christ. Whomever we meet, we will win them for Christ, so that they will also join us. We will send preaching teams to mountainous and faraway places where the gospel has not yet reached. We are already able to lead people in village after village to turn away from idols to Christ. They then burn up their idols after repentance and faith in Christ.

Such is the indomitable spirit of the leadership of the

house churches in the face of opposition from the official church and the Communist authorities.

It is important to understand the nature of persecution and what its real object is. Just as certainly as the church's conflict is not against flesh and blood, whether Communist or other, so persecution is not aimed at the church, but at Jesus. When Saul of Tarsus was breathing out threatenings and slaughter against the disciples of the Lord, Christ called to him, "Saul, Saul, why do you persecute me?" Persecuting the church is really persecuting Christ. There are churches, even under Marxist regimes, which are not being persecuted. There is so little true manifestation of the life of Jesus. But where the life of Jesus is very active, persecution is a present reality. Spiritual vigor among the people of God demands the close attention of the devil. There are many Christians whom the devil can well afford to leave alone because they are no danger to him.

Early in 1985 I asked a pastor in Hong Kong who was constantly in and out of China whether the great wave of blessing in the early eighties was being maintained. He replied that it was continuing, but that it had slowed down in many areas due to persecution. He felt that it was a good thing that the mass growth of a few years back had given way to a time of separation of the true from the false, and a time of consolidation. "The God of all grace . . . after you have suffered a little while, will himself restore you and make you strong, firm and steadfast."[38]

The issue of suffering for Christ is the big test of where a believer's heart really is. If it is down here on earth, the prospect of some heavenly reward "in the sweet by-and-by" has no big appeal. He wants instant deliverance from "the nasty now-and-now"! But if heaven has really captured his heart, if earthly things have faded in the light of eternal realities, his attitude to suffering radically changes. He finds he is able not only to rejoice but even to "leap for joy" as Jesus taught. The attitude to suffering is crucial. If believers have not come into victory in this area, hard times bring witnessing to a halt.

Apart from suffering's purifying and maturing effect on the church, it seems in some inexplicable way to release the

power of God, often with electrifying effect. The principle of
the cross at work in a yielded life can crack opposition, melt
the hardened heart, and open a tightly shut mind to the light
of truth. This has been demonstrated again and again in
China.

A letter written in 1982 from Henan province tells of ten
young people who, after earnest prayer, set out to preach. As
they proclaimed the gospel with tears, passers-by stopped to
listen, fortune-tellers (of whom there are many in China)
broke down and wept, and workers on their way home from
the factories forgot their hunger and stayed to listen, for
God's power was present. The large crowd would not let
them stop, tired though they were. Then came the Public
Security Bureau officials, who tied up the young preachers,
dragged them away, and beat them until they were
unconscious.

In the group was one girl who was only fourteen. When,
after being thus beaten, she revived and continued
witnessing, all kinds of people broke down, repented, and
believed in Jesus. The situation was similar for four of the
young men in the party. They were forced to kneel for three
days without food or water. Even as they were being beaten
until the blood flowed, they continued praying, singing, and
praising the Lord, until even their tormentors were
converted and believed the gospel. They could have looked
their officials in the face and boldly declared, "Death is at
work in us, but life is at work in you."[39]

The report concludes:

> So in this area recently, the flame of the Gospel has
> spread everywhere. There has never been a revival here
> before, but through the persecution, this place has truly
> the seeds of life. May everyone who hears of this give
> thanks and praise for the revival of the church in this
> area. In men's eyes, this is an unfortunate happening,
> but for Christians it is like a rich banquet. This lesson
> cannot be learned from books, and this sweetness is not
> usually tasted by men. This rich life does not exist in a
> comfortable environment. Where there is no cross there
> is no crown. If the spices are not refined to become oil,
> the fragrance of the perfume cannot flow forth; and if
> grapes are not crushed in the vat, they will not become
> wine.

Dear brethren, these saints who have gone down into the furnace, far from being harmed, have had their faces glorified and their spirits filled with power, with greater authority to preach the Word, and a far more abundant life. The Lord will have the final victory in their bodies, making Satan to be ashamed. In the end, Satan had no way of making these young preachers denounce their faith and they were released.

The great epistle on suffering in the New Testament is 1 Peter. There is nothing heavy or oppressive about this letter. In the very first chapter, addressing the saints who "have had to suffer grief in all kinds of trials," Peter assures them that as they believe, they "are filled with an inexpressible and glorious joy."[40] But that joy does not necessarily follow. Let me repeat: What suffering does for us is determined by our attitude to it. Peter has something vital to say on this subject:

"Therefore, since Christ suffered in his body, arm yourselves also with the same attitude, because he who has suffered in his body is done with sin. As a result, he does not live the rest of his earthly life for evil human desires, but rather for the will of God."[41] The attitude of our Lord is seen in the way in which He set His face to tread the path that led to Calvary. Suffering may destroy a believer. Hardship may cause him to pull back. Persecution may neutralize his testimony. That is usually Satan's purpose in mounting such attacks on the child of God. In Revelation, John recorded these words of Jesus: "Do not be afraid of what you are about to suffer. I tell you, the devil will put some of you in prison to test you, and you will suffer persecution for ten days. Be faithful, even to the point of death, and I will give you the crown of life."[42]

Peter teaches us that our protective armor against such attacks is a mind-set, a heart attitude, to accept the suffering that may be required of us in fulfilling the will of God. Peter was well qualified to speak on this score. He recalled how he and John had been arrested for preaching in the temple courts and brought before the Sanhedrin. They were asked in whose name they had healed the lame man. "It is by the name of Jesus Christ of Nazareth," answered Peter, "whom you crucified but whom God raised from the dead, that this

man stands before you completely healed."[43] When your
Master has been executed a few weeks before by these very
men, you don't answer them like that unless you have armed
yourself with a mind to suffer.

In the next chapter of Acts, all the apostles are arraigned
before the same body, flogged, and released only after being
threatened about speaking any more in the name of Jesus.
We are told, "The apostles left the Sanhedrin, rejoicing
because they had been counted worthy of suffering disgrace
for the Name. Day after day, in the temple courts and from
house to house, they never stopped teaching and
proclaiming the good news that Jesus is the Christ."[44] You
don't behave like that, however zealous, unless you are
armed with a mind to suffer.

Watchman Nee ministered on this very theme before the
Communist authorities shut him up in prison for twenty
years. God was surely preparing him, as he was preparing
the flock, for what lay ahead. He strongly emphasized that
God is not against enjoyment, and will not withhold any
good thing from His obedient children; but that does not
prevent us from having a mind to suffer.

> There is much suffering that we can avoid if we wish:
> but if we are to be of use to the Lord, it is a fundamental
> necessity that we make deliberate choice of the path of
> suffering for His sake. Unless we acquire a disposition
> to suffer for Him, the work we do will be of a very
> superficial quality . . . The question is not one of the
> amount of suffering we may be called upon to meet, but
> of our attitude toward it . . . Suffering may not be your
> daily portion, but you must daily be prepared to suffer.[45]

We do not know how much suffering Watchman Nee was
called upon to bear, but we do know he never denied his Lord
or chose the easy path of compromise to escape from prison.
David Adeney describes the same unshakeable commitment
in Wang Mingdao:

> Of the same spirit was the courageous Wang Mingdao.
> He had seen clearly that even the smallest compromise
> would open the way for further retreats from the truth.
> For him, loyalty to Jesus Christ had to have precedence
> over all other loyalty. Obedience to the demands of

Jesus Christ inevitably brought him in conflict with the
secular state. He knew full well that the course he was
taking could only lead to prison, and his bag was
always packed for the time when the call should come.[46]

There was nothing fatalistic about that packed bag.
Wang knew that God could deliver him, but God had given
him no intimation that He would save him by a supernatural
deliverance from what many of his compatriots were
suffering. Every time he saw that packed bag it would
strengthen the determination in his heart: "I will not shrink
from this path. I have a mind to suffer." It was like this with
the three Hebrews faced with the fiery furnace. The God
they served was able to deliver them. "But even if He does
not," they said, "we will not serve . . . the image of
gold . . ."[47] It's that little "but if not" clause that represents
the mind to suffer.

Perhaps we feel this would all be very relevant if we were
living, like the Chinese church, under a Communist regime.
But how can it apply to Christians brought up in the freedom
of the West? Are we to pray for persecution, court calamity,
or indulge in some self-inflicted suffering? No indeed. But
we are mistaken if we think that having a democratic
government can guarantee us freedom from persecution. It
is not only the civil authorities who persecute.

I believe that for some years God has been warning His
children in the West through what has been happening in
Russia, China, and Ethiopia, as well as in certain Islamic
and other non-Marxist societies. Persecution for the child of
God is a reality, even in the twentieth century, and we must
not fool ourselves that it can never happen to us. I fear that if
it did overtake us in our present state, the spiritual casualty
rate would be high.

In China the issue is clear-cut: to live for Jesus without
compromise and confess Him without fear is to suffer. For us
in the West this is not necessarily so. How then is it really
possible in our situation to have a mind to suffer? In what
ways are we to embrace the cross? These are questions that
we must now face.

13

HOW TO EMBRACE THE CROSS

Therefore, since we have so great a crowd of witnesses surrounding us ... let us run with endurance the race ... fixing our eyes on Jesus ... who for the joy set before him endured the cross.
Hebrews 12:1-2 (NASB)

A brilliant young Chinese scientist, converted to Christ while a student in the U.S., wrote to David Adeney shortly before returning to his native Shanghai:

> I do not care whether I live six days or six years. I can only say with the apostle Paul, "I do not count my life of any value, nor as precious to myself, if only I may accomplish my course and the ministry I have received from the Lord Jesus, to testify to the Gospel of the grace of God."[48]

This young man, living in the easy affluence of the West and far removed from the kind of persecution that he knew he would face back in China, had heard the call of God, and adopted a mind to suffer. To do the same is within the grasp of everyone who reads this book.

Soldiers off the battlefield may be able to perform their duties without any great hardship or self-denial. But on the battlefield hardship is a daily fact of life. For this reason soldiers have to taste something of the rigors of the battlefield in their training. In the early days of World War II some Allied troops in North Africa, where I was serving, suffered badly when they at length faced their "baptism of fire." They had been pampered by peacetime conditions. They were soft-bellied and vulnerable. That's the way it is with many of Christ's soldiers.

The church in China calls out to us, "Arm yourselves with a mind to suffer." If you wait until you hear the zip of bullets or the crack of exploding shells, you have waited too long. Don't wait for suffering or persecution to overtake you. Now is the time to get into training.

We must not think of soldiers of Christ as comprising only the elite of the kingdom of God. The New Testament takes it for granted that every true believer is a soldier. To be saved is to be drafted, and you cannot separate soldiering from suffering. Paul, the seasoned warrior, reminds Timothy, his young aide, "Take your share of suffering as a good soldier of Christ Jesus."[49] Suffering was something that Timothy could either avoid or embrace. That's how it is with us. Is it going to take a Communist revolution to make us disciplined soldiers of Christ?

The Corinthian church was rich in spiritual gifts, but poor in self-discipline. Paul uses the figure of the Olympic games to illustrate his own experience:

> Do you not know that in a race all the runners compete, but only one receives the prize? So run that you may obtain it. Every athlete exercises self-control in all things. They do it to receive a perishable wreath, but we an imperishable. Well, I do not run aimlessly, I do not box as one beating the air; but I pommel my body and subdue it, lest after preaching to others I myself should be disqualified.[50]

There are many Christians who are flabby due to overeating and under-exercising. The physical is all too often a reflection of the spiritual. Says Paul, "I pommel my body"—that is, "I give it a hard time because I want to be able to endure hardness." God is not looking for us all to become fitness addicts. You can be an enthusiast for physical exercise and still fail to "subdue" the body, or "make it your slave," in the way Paul means here.

It is not only on the track that the athlete trains but also at the meal table. He avoids overeating and late rising. Many Christians visibly wilt if called upon to sacrifice their creature comforts and endure a little hardship in the work of God. Others who are not generally self-indulgent still have weak spots, where they regularly give in to some fad of the body. If you're aiming for gold in the Olympics, you can't afford that weak spot. It must be "self-control in *all things*," Paul says. With most of us there are practical issues in which we need to take ourselves in hand. Jesus taught us that if we really want to shoulder the cross, we must learn to say "no" to self.[51]

Many of us do not seem to realize that we have a war on our hands. In the face of those insatiable appetites that "wage war against the soul,"[52] our policy is to give in rather than dig in. It's time we quit treating our self-indulgences as a bit of a joke, and begin to take this teaching of Paul seriously. It is time for pommeling that body of ours and putting it through its paces. This is an aspect of growing up.

Paul does not advocate the path of asceticism, which implies that the body is inherently sinful and must be constantly punished. It is not a call to exchange a nightshirt for a hairshirt! It is true that God "richly provides us with everything for our enjoyment," but enjoyment is not to become indulgence. That happens when the body unseats the spirit and takes over the saddle. The vital question is, "Who is in control?"

For the athlete in training the issue is very simple. He knows that if the body has not learned to take orders off the track, it will not respond to orders on the track, and that supreme effort will not come forth when it is needed. Watchman Nee earned the right to speak on this matter. In an address to his fellow workers he said this:

> Brothers and sisters, if you have not yet brought your body under control, you had better call a halt in the work and gain dominion over it before you try to exercise authority in any wider realm. You may take great pleasure in the work, but it will have little value if you are dominated by your physical cravings. Serving the Lord is not a mere matter of preaching sermons from the platform. Paul knew that.[53]

There is a New Testament ruggedness many of these Chinese Christians have developed that makes our Western Christianity look a little anemic. Take this report from Inner Mongolia, where three pastors in their seventies were released from labor camps. All of them had served in excess of twenty years. But they were just thrilled to serve God among the house churches. Said one of them: "We are old, but not too old to baptize. Our last baptismal service was held in a freezing pond. The Lord enabled us to stay in the water for almost an hour!" I wonder how many converts the three of them baptized in an hour!

This pommeling of the body may be a little painful, but it enables us to have the mind to suffer, as Jesus did. In this our Lord showed the perfect balance. We may be sure that He enjoyed His meal when He sat to eat with the tax gatherers and the sinners. He certainly wasn't an ascetic. He wasn't even a teetotaler. This gave the Pharisees the opportunity to accuse Him of excess, calling Him"a glutton and a drunkard." The truth was, He never failed to exercise the most exemplary control over His body.

Hungry and weary at Sychar's well, Jesus refused the disciples' invitation to take food. There was a spiritual harvest, fully ripe for the reaping, so even the cry of the body for food must be made to wait. "I have food to eat," He explained to His disciples, "that you know nothing about."[54]

In the Garden of Gethsemane Jesus called to His disciples to watch and pray with Him. That meant saying "no" to the craving for sleep. As so often happens with us, they went to sleep. "The spirit is willing but the body is weak," said Jesus.[55] Watchman Nee asks the pertinent question, "What is the good of a willing spirit, if the body is weak? If you are to watch with the Lord when He requires it, you will need a willing body as well as a willing spirit."[56] That means a body that has been disciplined, that has been buffeted into submission and readily responds to the dictates of your spirit.

This emphasis on the believer's need to embrace the cross, so strongly brought out in the New Testament epistles, seems hardly to find a place in Christian teaching today. Is it that we have graduated from all that, and are now into the much more exciting and attractive teaching about prosperity? If we have faith, we are told, we can escape from the "poverty trap" and enjoy material abundance. This teaching is not altogether wrong, but it has a lopsided emphasis. It seriously lacks the balance of the cross of which the New Testament is so full. If we believe that the wealth of the nations is to flow to the church, this teaching is not intended to produce a generation of wealthy Christians.

The New Testament does not teach that poverty is a crippling curse and that to escape from it must be a spiritual priority. How was it that the One who became poor for us, who had "nowhere to lay His head," who had to ask for a penny from the congregation to illustrate His point, did not seem to have this "prosperity" faith? And how could Paul speak of being so content "whether well fed or hungry, whether living in plenty or in want"?[57] Poverty is only a trap when we face it with a lack of faith. The apostle faced his times of want with the same glad submission and buoyant faith he had in his times of abundance. He had to prove God to be true in both experiences.

Paul was certainly not speaking disparagingly of his apostolic ministry, but rather commending it, when he said, "To this very hour we go hungry and thirsty, we are in rags, we are brutally treated, we are homeless."[58] I wonder if there are any budding apostles around who eagerly aspire to this sort of apostolic qualification!

When Paul prayed for deliverance from his "thorn in the flesh"—whatever that was—God said to him, "My grace is sufficient for you, for my power is made perfect in weakness."[59] Here it comes again, the embracing of the cross that brings a release of the power of God. "Therefore," says Paul, "I will boast all the more gladly about my weaknesses, so that Christ's power may rest on me. That is why, for Christ's sake, I delight in weaknesses, in insults, in hardships, in persecutions, in difficulties."[60]

"Just a moment, Paul, what you really mean is that you are willing to put up with them while you call on the Lord for speedy deliverance."

"No, I don't. I mean what I said. I *delight* in weaknesses, in insults, in hardships, in persecutions, in difficulties. For when I am weak, then I am strong."

We hear it said that any testings, trials, and pressures that come upon us do not come from God and are not designed to perfect us. We are told not to entertain any idea that such are among the "all things that work together for good." Rather, we should take the view that such trials are an attack of Satan, and call on the Lord to deliver us immediately. Faith for instant deliverance is the only course. Faith to endure does not seem to be an option.

Is this the teaching in either the Old or New Testament? Take the heroes of faith listed in Hebrews 11. Not all get a mention in the record because of the faith of their achievement; some are listed because of the faith of their endurance. By faith some "escaped the edge of the sword," while others, equally men of faith, were "put to death by the sword." There were those who "went about in sheepskins and goatskins, destitute, persecuted and mistreated."[61] Hardly a good advertisement for material prosperity, or for deliverance from "testings, trials, and pressures," yet the inspired writer reserves for them this final accolade: "the world was not worthy of them."

Paul recounts the hardships he and his fellow workers suffered in the province of Asia. He says, "We were under great pressure, far beyond our ability to endure, so that we despaired even of life." But he saw the benefit of this in the outworking of the cross in their lives, and in their coming into a greater dependence on God, for he goes on, "Indeed, in our hearts we felt the sentence of death. But this happened that we might not rely on ourselves but on God, who raises the dead. He has delivered us from such a deadly peril, and he will deliver us. On him we have set our hope that he will continue to deliver us."[62] There was no instant deliverance here; instead, great endurance was needed.

It is our love of a smooth, trouble-free ride that causes us to shrink from the cross of Christ. If we are going to shoulder a cross at all, we want it planed and polished, not the "old rugged cross" that Jesus bore. That sort chafes the shoulder and leaves splinters in the fingers. No, it is not poverty that hinders us from embracing the cross, but our affluence and the materialistic spirit that so often goes with it.

Very few Chinese believers are materially prosperous. Many are very poor, even by Chinese standards. But I believe that the Head of the church says to them, as He said to the suffering church of Smyrna: "I know your afflictions

and your poverty—yet you are rich!"[63]   This is surely true
New Testament prosperity. "Has not God chosen those who
are poor in the eyes of the world to be," not materially
wealthy, but "rich in faith and to inherit the kingdom...?"[64]

If we were presented with a choice, would we prefer to be
like the Smyrnans, rich in faith but materially poor, or like
the Laodiceans, poor in faith but materially rich? "When it
comes to spiritual or material wealth," someone would be
quick to tell us, "it doesn't have to be 'either/or;' it should be
both." For some this may be true, but did the Father give His
Son that option? Did the Christians who were told in the
Hebrew epistle, "you . . . joyfully accepted the confiscation of
your property," have that option?   Their joy was not
"because you have faith for those goods to be speedily
replaced, and even more to be given you," but "because you
knew that you yourselves had better and lasting
possessions."[65]

"Prosperity," we are told, "is not to make us rich for
ourselves, but that we might be rich toward God and give
generously to His work." Fine, but how many Christians
respond to this because their single motive is to give more,
and how many because it also holds out the prospect of
improving their own living standards? The gift of giving in
the New Testament, mentioned alongside such gifts as
prophesying, serving, and teaching,[66] is a faith ministry
that does not need to operate out of abundance.

The greatest givers in Scripture, according to heaven's
estimate, were materially poor. Take the widow who put her
"two mites" into the treasury. It was "all she had to live on,"
and no one would ever have known, if Jesus had not revealed
it. But it was He who said that she had given more than all
the rich.[67] Or the Macedonian Christians of whom Paul
said, "Out of the most severe trial, their overflowing joy and
their extreme poverty welled up in rich generosity. For I
testify that they gave as much as they were able, and even
beyond their ability. Entirely on their own, they urgently
pleaded with us for the privilege of sharing in this service to
the saints."[68] That's the kind of giving that makes heaven
sit up and take notice, and you'll find more of it in China
than in the affluent West.

If God gives us material wealth as we seek first His kingdom, then that is good. There will be grace to use it rightly, to advance the kingdom and not wither our spiritual life. In itself wealth is not a goal of faith to be sought. It can be a dangerous teaching if no mention is made of the many biblical warnings about the love of riches. And those who append to their teaching an appeal for funds—"Give to this work of mine, and see how God will prosper you!"—must not be surprised if their motives are questioned.

To live simply and modestly in an affluent society is costly. It takes the cross of Christ to put to death that acquisitive spirit, and to bring us into a place of contentment. Paul warned Timothy of those "who think that godliness is a means to financial gain," and went on to say that "if we have food and clothing"—please note the "if"—"we will be content with that."[69]

There is another vital area where we may, if we will, embrace the cross. Bodily suffering may not be our lot just now, but mental suffering is always with us, and some Christians cannot cope with it. Solomon reminds us, if we should need reminding, that ". . . rash words . . . are like sword thrusts."[70] Thoughtless behavior may wound deeply. Unchristian attitudes may cause grievous suffering. All that has been said about bodily suffering applies equally to mental suffering. What it does to you and in you; what, if anything, it accomplishes for the kingdom of God, depends upon the way you respond to it.

We cannot avoid being hurt. It is an occupational hazard of living in an imperfect world. But there is nothing accidental about it. It is part of God's providential ordering of our lives, and therefore contains potential blessing. "Those who suffer according to God's will"—that is, suffering that is not the result of our own sin or stupidity— "should commit themselves to their faithful Creator and continue to do good."[71]

Where there is a failure to arm yourself with a mind to suffer, words, actions, and attitudes that cause suffering become a battleground for defeat instead of victory. Your unseemly reactions become as unspiritual as the words and actions that cause them; and Satan wins a two-fold victory.

The wound quickly becomes infected with hurt pride, anger, and resentment. If you still do not take action, bitterness, self-pity, and unforgiveness will set in.

From then on, everything that the one who hurt you says or does is viewed with a jaundiced eye. You don't want to hear anything good about him. Any success he has will only be "temporary." Any kindness he performs will have a "dubious motive." Nothing that he does will be right. Your judgment will be warped by your own prejudices.

These hurts are in most cases a mere pinprick compared with what many Chinese believers have suffered. Are you thinking that it must be easier to take persecutions from the world than to take hurts from your fellow Christians, or from those who are particularly close? But these are the very hurts that many of the saints in China have experienced. Unfortunately, not all believers there have been faithful to God and to their brothers and sisters in Christ. There have been many betrayals, and many accusations of believers by believers.

Many a pastor or preacher has been dragged before a public meeting convened to accuse him to find that some of his own flock, even those whom he led to Christ, were there to speak against him in front of the unbelieving Communists. Watchman Nee and Wang Mingdao experienced it. And it wasn't only leaders who suffered in this way. Many ordinary believers were betrayed by fellow Christians, and it was not just humiliation and public dishonoring that they had to suffer. There often followed years in jail or labor camp, separated from family and loved ones. Plenty of time to let the gall of it get into your soul, if you allowed that to happen. That so many came through with a beautiful Christ-like spirit was only because they had armed themselves with "a mind to suffer."

There is nothing more destructive of relationships in the body of Christ than the harmful way in which Christians often react to hurts, usually thoughtlessly, maliciously. God is calling us to get into training, to have a mind to suffer for His sake—to embrace the cross. But how do we do it? Peter and Paul were well qualified to answer.

1. Make sure that your suffering is not something you

have foolishly brought on yourself. There is no value in that kind of suffering.[72]

2. If you suffer because you are a Christian, you are to praise God that you bear His name. You are suffering in His will, and you can commit your cause to Him.[73]

3. Do not let suffering of whatever sort take you by surprise, or think it strange. Rejoice in the privilege of sharing in Christ's sufferings. You are not being singled out for special punishment but for special blessing. The Spirit of glory is resting on you.[74]

4. Take your eyes off the cause of the suffering, and become conscious of God working in the situation. You are following in the footsteps of Christ.[75]

5. When you suffer for right, you may be hurt but you cannot be harmed. You are, in fact, blessed. Seize the opportunity this may bring to witness.[76]

6. Don't retaliate or seek vengeance, but, even as Jesus did, commit the issues to God, who judges justly.[77]

7. Don't develop a "martyr" spirit or join in the "pity party." View your suffering as a small thing. What is it in comparison with Christ's suffering? How does it even compare with Paul's and his fellow workers', which he described as "our light and momentary troubles"! Get taken up with the "eternal glory that far outweighs them all."[78]

8. Aim at coming to that place where you can say with Paul, "I delight in all these sufferings because in this kind of weakness I am really strong."[79]

Was Paul not referring to the marks of suffering when he closed his epistle to the Galatians with these words: "I bear on my body the marks of Jesus"? Do you bear any mark of suffering?

Hast thou no wound?
Yet I was wounded by the archers, spent,
Lean me against a tree to die; and rent
By ravening beasts that compassed me, I swooned;
Hast thou no wound?

Hast thou no scar?
No hidden scar on foot or side or hand?
I hear thee sung as mighty in the land,
I hear them hail thy bright ascendant star,
Hast thou no scar?

No wound? No scar?
Yet, as the Master shall the servant be,
And pierced are the feet that follow me;
But thine are whole: can he have followed far
Who has no wound nor scar?

Amy Carmichael

14

DYNAMIC PRAYING

After they prayed, the place where they were meeting was shaken. And they were all filled with the Holy Spirit and spoke the word of God boldly.

Acts 4:31

This early record gives us some challenging insights into the prayer life of the first Christians. Not only was the early church born from the womb of prayer, but by prayer was fed and nurtured. It was on their knees that they met those first blasts of the enemy's counterattack, whether persecution from without or dissension from within. The church in China was also born out of prayer, and sacrificial praying has characterized it from the start.

Pastor Hsi was a contemporary of the early missionary pioneers like Hudson Taylor. He was a Confucian scholar and an opium addict when God saved him. From the time of his conversion and deliverance from opium addiction, he adopted the name Sheng-mo, meaning "conqueror of demons," in the conviction that what God had done for him he would, by God's grace, do for others.

Within a few months of his own deliverance his wife, as yet unconverted, became uncontrollably demonized. Hsi called for a fast for three days and nights in his household. He then laid hands on his wife, and in the name of Jesus commanded the evil spirits to depart and torment her no more. Mrs. Hsi was delivered instantly and permanently, and became his devoted partner in the work.

From then on, conflict with the powers of darkness was

very much the characteristic of this man's ministry. The power of Satan let loose against him was great, but God's power to save, deliver, and heal was greater. Churches were established throughout the whole region as a result of his ministry. Whatever the crisis—the need of divine guidance or wisdom, the deliverance of opium addicts or those otherwise demonized, the withstanding of opposition—Hsi had only one solution. He gave himself to prayer and fasting. What mighty victories and deliverances God wrought for him and through him!

God caused the church in China to flex her prayer muscles and to prove Him by remarkable answers to prayer in the prerevolutionary period. Watchman Nee tells a story of how, in the early days of the work, he and six other brothers went on a preaching tour to an island off the southern China coast.

There was little response to their preaching. Wu was the youngest in the team, only sixteen and newly converted. He asked the crowd why they would not believe. They replied that they already had a god, Ta-wang (meaning Great King). For centuries they celebrated his festival every January on a day revealed by divination. It was always a perfectly fine day. On learning that the festival was fixed for January 11, in two days' time, Wu boldly declared: "I promise you it will rain on the eleventh."

"That is enough!" retorted the crowd. "We don't want to hear any more preaching. If there is rain on the eleventh, then your God is God!"

The news spread like wildfire. Wu's rash prediction had put the older Christians, Watchman Nee included, on the spot. They stopped their preaching and gave themselves to prayer. God gave Watchman Nee the words, "Where is the God of Elijah?" He now felt assured that God would send rain on the eleventh. They thanked God and went out to broadcast their acceptance of the devil's challenge.

That evening, as doubts began to assail them, they went back to prayer. "We want rain now, Lord." Again the word came, "Where is the God of Elijah?" They felt rebuked. They confessed their sin of unbelief and acknowledged that they did not need rain until the time of the procession, eight o'clock in the morning on the eleventh.

On the morning of the eleventh Watchman Nee was awakened by the rays of the sun. It was already past seven o'clock. "This isn't rain, Lord. Please send the rain!"

Back came the word, "Where is the God of Elijah?"

Humbled, he walked silently down to breakfast. Everyone was very quiet as they took their place at the table. There was not a cloud in the sky. As they bowed to say grace, they reminded God of His promise, and before they could say "Amen" they heard the first drops of rain on the tiles. There was a steady shower as they took their first bowl of rice.

In the village, some of the younger generation looked at that first shower and said, "There is God. No more Ta-wang! He is kept in by the rain." But the faithful brought him out on a sedan chair. Surely he would stop the rain. Back at the breakfast table the team said grace again for the second bowl of rice. This time they asked God for heavier rain. Before their breakfast was finished it was coming down in bucketfuls, and the street was deep in water.

The procession had only proceeded a few yards when the coolies stumbled and fell. Poor Ta-wang had his jaw and left arm fractured. Emergency repairs were quickly carried out. Slipping and stumbling, the coolies carried him halfway around the village; then the floods defeated them. Some of the village elders, bareheaded and without umbrellas because of their faith in Ta-wang's weather, had also fallen and were in serious difficulty—in more ways than one!

The idol was taken into a home where they "divined" that they had gotten the day wrong. January 14 at six o'clock in the evening was the proper time for the procession. "Lord, send rain on the fourteenth, but give us four good days until then," the workers prayed. That very afternoon the skies cleared, and the weather was fine for the next few days. The fourteenth dawned, bright and clear. Again at the appointed time they reminded God of His promises. Not a minute late, the answer came with torrential rain and floods. The power of Ta-wang was broken.[80]

Undoubtedly the pressure of persecution had deepened and intensified the prayer life of the Chinese church. It was a slow process which began after the terrible 1966-69 period of the Cultural Revolution. A few servants of God, moved by the spiritual desolation they faced, began to pray for revival. They urged others to cast off their fears and do the same. These small secret prayer groups grew into Spirit-filled house churches. Deprived of "ordained" leaders, "lay" leaders rose up to take their place. The Spirit of God was moving all over China, and house churches sprang up in every city and town and in countless villages. The new Chinese church, again, was born from the womb of prayer.

In a coastal city in 1967 the resumption of small meetings had brought a time of intense opposition and persecution. Over a period of three months the churches were called by their pastors to engage in prayer and fasting. Believers were being humiliated, tortured, and threatened. Many died in prison, while others were killed or crippled by savage beatings. Then in 1978 a powerful work of the Holy Spirit brought thousands to Christ. One city reports 50,000 Christians meeting in 600 households, which constitutes one in eight, or 12.5 percent of the population. Even children remained true to the Lord despite being threatened by their teachers.

According to the United Nations' latest estimate, one out of three people in China are under fifteen. That means that there are about 300 million children in China. No wonder the authorities insist that no one under eighteen is allowed to attend church or be taught the gospel.

Christian children at a very early age have to learn how to protect their parents and families. "Whenever a stranger stepped into our home," said a five-year-old to a staff member of Christian Communications, "I would see if he was for us or against us."

"How could you tell?" she asked the child.

"I'll pray and the Lord will tell me," was the answer.

"How do you pray?" was the next question.

Smiling, the little girl replied, "Oh, you won't know when I am praying because I pray in my heart."

There was a Christian lady who returned from overseas to her native village in 1974, fearful of what she might find. She found eight rejoicing believers with a strong pure faith. Those who had been sent to prison had witnessed to other prisoners. Prayer and fasting were normal activities in the village, and God was demonstrating his power to heal, confounding the skepticism of the unbelievers.

In some communities Christians meet every day to pray for their country. Those who have been privileged to meet with them speak of the spirit of urgency that characterizes their praying. Quite unlikely converts become praying saints. Take the case of the old man who had been troubled by a demon. After the demon was cast out he turned to the Lord and became a dedicated believer. He deeply desired to serve the Lord, but was told there was little he could do. Then he began to rise at four o'clock every morning to pray. Now he recognizes that this is the ministry to which God has called him.

One who has researched the growth of the house churches describes the "disciplined prayer life" of believers as its distinguishing feature. There is nothing inward-looking or self-centered about the way they pray. Their prayer life reaches around the world. In one of China's most important cities a group meets every Saturday from nine in the morning till three or later in the afternoon for a time of prayer and fasting. On this occasion their primary request was that Bible schools and seminaries in the West would remain true to the Word of God.

Here are some sample prayer requests from a house church:

> May the Lord enable me to have spiritual wisdom to expound the gospel clearly and fully. Oh, for the gift of raising high the cross! Oh, for the power of the Holy Spirit when preaching the cross, that all men may be drawn to the Lord by the power of the cross!
>
> May the Lord give preaching ability to expose sin, to make men fear. And the help of the Spirit that men may be convicted of sin and righteousness and judgment, and so earnestly repent.
>
> May the Lord continually place a spirit of awe in my heart, that I may obtain humility, and also grow daily in wisdom and knowledge.
>
> May the Lord grant me by His grace the ability to obey His Holy Spirit so that I can strengthen my brethren.

For the gift of establishing and pastoring the church
and for prophetic preaching.
For the fullness of the Spirit.
For a willingness to suffer.
May the Lord control my tongue to speak words that
will build up others.
May the Lord enable me not to love the world or its
empty glory, but to be bold and be completely committed
to God.
May I have the gift of praising God and of spiritual
songs.

I spoke earlier of the revival in Henan province. It seems
that God is continuing to confirm His word with signs and
wonders. Although the majority of believers are farmers
and ordinary peasants, many Communist Party members,
cadres, brigade leaders and other officials are turning to
Christ. With many it is the result of miracles.

The people of Henan are very simple, honest, and frank.
These are qualities that make it easier for them to receive the
gospel. When they pray they take everything, great or small,
to the Lord, believing for an answer. In one village there was
a plague of rats that brought much destruction and sickness.
The Christians prayed and within days all the rats
mysteriously died.

Many people who have had terminal illnesses have been
healed through the prayers of Christians. One brother,
known to a Hong Kong pastor with whom I spoke, was
paralyzed and bedridden for many years before his
salvation. After receiving Christ he was totally healed, and
recently traveled the long road to Guanzhou to pick up
Bibles. It was here he met brothers from Hong Kong to
whom he told his story.

David Wang, brought up in Shanghai, recalls the
neighbor who had a little house built in her garden when she
became a Christian. This was used by visiting pastors as a
"prophets' chamber," but it was also used as a place for
fasting and prayer. "I remember Christians," recalls David,
"including my mother, who would go to 'the little ark,' as it
was called, and for days they would pray and fast. Even as a
young boy I would sense the fervency of their prayers—a
fervency that has never left China's Christians."

On a recent visit to China with a co-worker, David visited a lady who had just been released after twenty-three years in prison. They brought her food, medicine, clothing, money, and of course a Bible. "That woman was a saint!" recalled David. Before they left she requested prayer with the visitors. Very softly she began to pray. They felt as though "the ions and molecules of the atmosphere were suddenly charged." It seemed as though they could "sense the vibrations of the presence of God."

David was reminded of the first Christians: "After they prayed, the place where they were meeting was shaken." They could sense the moving and the shaking in the spiritual realm, as though this little woman was attacking the very gates of hell. "Though she prayed so softly, she was perspiring all over. We were immersed in an atmosphere of grace, communion, and intercession in spiritual warfare. She was reminding God of His promises and pledging her obedience to His word." Awed, they left the room of her little shack, as though they had been in the vestibule of heaven.

Without doubt, here in the West we are seeing God moving by His Holy Spirit. Many of us have become accustomed to attending celebrations and conventions that would be described as "charismatic." Generally, the atmosphere has been good, the worship lively, and the gifts of the Spirit in evidence. The preaching of the Word has been blessed, even anointed. Conversions, healings, and deliverances have been witnessed. But the whole operation has been largely man-centered, need-centered, and result-centered. We have looked to the charisma of the speaker to "draw in the net" and produce results, with the help of counselors. The measure of visible blessing may vary, but the manner of the Spirit's operation has become predictable. We almost know beforehand what will happen and we now have a generation of believers who don't expect anything more.

Isn't the vital missing element that awesome, subduing, melting, overwhelming Presence, that undefinable element that transforms a meeting from man-centeredness to God-centeredness? It lifts it from the mundane to the sublime, and from the expected to the spontaneous and unpredictable. It may release God's people into rhapsodies of praise, in which they feel as though they have joined the angelic choirs. Or it may prostrate them on their faces in an awed silence at the presence of His Majesty. Anxiety about results will then be far from their thinking. All will be consumed with God. It will be enough to know that He who is "majestic in holiness, awesome in glory, working wonders"[81] has taken the field.

Who will deny that this is the God of the Bible? This is how He has come again and again in Scripture and in history. Why do we so rarely experience it? Isn't it because we know so little about the kind of praying described in this chapter? The leaders just don't have time. They are much too busy with their schedules and their programs. And the people, who take their cue from the leaders, are likewise caught up in a busy round of activities. No one has time for this kind of praying.

If we are ever to know the presence of the God of majesty and might we must adjust our thinking and discover where our priorities really lie. The Holy Spirit wants to lead us into dynamic praying, but before this can happen we must let Him destroy our self-satisfaction with what we are currently seeking. The basis of such a rediscovery of God is holy discontent and "heart" hunger. "You will seek me and find me when you seek me *with all your heart.*" [82]

15

INTENSE HUNGER

Your statutes are wonderful; therefore I
obey them. The entrance of your words
gives light; it gives understanding to the
simple. I open my mouth and pant,
longing for your commands.
                                   Psalm 119:129-131

A young refugee from China who had found Christ in the
People's Republic two years before was asked by Paul
Kauffman whether he owned a Bible.

"No," he replied.

"A New Testament?"

"No."

"Did you have any Christian literature as a new
convert?"

"Yes. An old lady who was a Christian tore one page out
of her daily devotional book and gave it to me."[83]

Here is the first reason for the intense hunger of Chinese
believers for the word of God—the acute lack of Bibles and
Christian literature. It is a strange fact of life that we do not
value many of the precious things we have until we find
ourselves deprived of them. Here in the West we have a
superabundance of Bibles; most of us have two or three, with
Christian literature of every conceivable kind. How much do
we really value it all?

Here is a recent letter from a northwestern province
signed by one who calls himself Brother Zhu:

> The Spirit of the Lord has fallen upon us in these last
> days. Many of our young people have been filled with
> the Holy Spirit and are willing to dedicate their lives to

God. We cannot but give thanks to God. This last time
when we met in a certain county 125 people received
water baptism, and about 600 came to our gatherings.
Today our congregation registers about 1,000. The Holy
Spirit works mightily. It is difficult for me to describe
the urgency of the needs here. When the people see and
hear the Word of God, there are tears of joy flowing
down many of their faces. Their joy is beyond what
words could express.

The other factor behind this hunger is the powerful
moving of the Holy Spirit. Hunger for God is a hallmark of
revival, and wherever there is hunger for God there is hunger
for His Word. It is the work of the Holy Spirit to break down
our complacency and lethargy and give us a spiritual hunger
for the things of God. "Oh no, not another meeting!" is a
comment often thought, if not expressed, among Western
Christians. In the Chinese house churches you will hear the
eager question, "When is the next meeting?"

In many places Bibles are too scarce and too precious
even to be taken to the Christian gatherings. A
government raid on the meeting place is always a
danger, so all that is brought to the meeting is
notebooks into which the Scriptures are hand-copied.

Before the Revolution, God had raised up in China a
number of great teachers and evangelists like John Sung,
Wang Mingdao, and Watchman Nee. Their ministry,
however, was similar to that of men in the West with a fine
pulpit ministry, holding captive large congregations who
came week by week to be fed. But the situation in China has
changed all that. The great men have all been arrested. The
great names have gone. The church in the house has
compelled the whole body of Christ to function. In place of
the big preacher, God is raising up a multitude of new
ministries, teachers, and preachers. A house church will
often devote one night a week to learning the art of
preaching or how to share the gospel with others.

All this does not mean that they do not highly value the
visits of those who have an anointed ministry in the Word of
God. Rather the reverse, as the following reveals:

A preacher was invited for the day to a small town to
hold meetings. At dawn, the building was crammed
with 600 people, with others packed into the courtyard
outside. They were willing to suffer the extremely cold
weather in order to hear the Lord's message. Before the
preacher arrived they sang hymns in order to prepare
their hearts to receive the word of God. The preacher
spoke three times and the Christians sat and listened
from early morning until late at night. Still they did not
want to disperse. They plucked his sleeve, saying, "We
have never heard such good preaching." They were
extraordinarily eager to hear Bible truth expounded.

One itinerant preacher recounted how, when asked what
his subject was, he replied, "About Jesus Christ in the book
of Matthew."

"Oh," they replied, "he is going to preach the book of
Matthew. The entire book is about Jesus Christ!" They held
him to his word. Thirty-seven hours later he finshed a verse-
by-verse exposition of the life of Jesus Christ in the book of
Matthew.[84]

A sister in Christ who was able to spend a good deal of
time in China between 1980 and 1982, a period when there
was rapid expansion among the house churches, tells how
she attended an ordination service in a house church. There
were twelve pastors and house church leaders present. They
were ordaining a farmer from the countryside who had been
converted in 1962 by reading a Bible loaned to him by an
elderly Christian woman. She eventually gave him the
Bible, fearing that the Red Guards might find it and burn it,
as this was the time of the Cultural Revolution.

As the believers grew in number, the farmer saw that
teaching was as important as evangelizing. With only a few
Bibles in the whole village, how were the people to be taught?
He was led to compile a topical Bible handbook, which took
him seven years to complete. It took so long because every
time his then-unconverted wife found the book she would
tear it up or burn it. In addition to that difficulty, the only
time for writing was between the end of his daily work and
sunset, as they had no electricity in the country. On
completion the book was mimeographed by the believers,
and 10,000 copies had been distributed in ten prefectures

within that province. The pastors and leaders felt that this man had qualified for ordination!

The same sister heard an itinerant preacher from Shanghai tell of his visit to a village in Henan province. He was a stranger there. Some of the villagers took him to their home, into a room with Scriptures plastered all over the walls. They wanted to share the gospel with him. When they found out he was a Christian they immediately asked him to preach. They took him to a room where another preacher was concluding his message to 400 or more people. The congregation was overflowing into the yard. He took over and preached from nine in the morning till eleven at night. Then the believers asked him to spend the night at an elderly woman's house and preach again the next day.

He was awakened in the middle of the night and given a full breakfast at four in the morning. Then they rushed him to another meeting which was to start at six o'clock. To satisfy their great hunger for God's Word without disrupting production the believers will often gather together hours before they work, and then again hours after they finish.

The preacher reported that in this particular village, Christians will hang posters on their doors to proclaim their faith in Christ.   He saw only three doors without posters. These, he was told, were the homes of former landlords who were still hesitant to be bold in their testimony because of their "bad record." He was told that even the Public Security Chief was a secret believer, and would not persecute the Christians.

When you get this kind of hunger for the Word of God, you have no need to fear how people will respond when that Word is brought to them. Wang Mingdao was not released from prison until 1980 at eighty years of age. He had spent twenty-four years in prison. David Wang visited him in his little room in Shanghai. He was already half-blind and in feeble health, suffering from a number of illnesses. David asked this Mr. Valiant-for-Truth why it was that the church in China was experiencing "such magnificent and glorious interventions by God." "Well," he said, "we have no Bible, no church, no missionaries, no Bible schools, no seminaries. Perhaps it is because we have nothing that God has special mercy on us. He has given us the faith of a mustard seed, simple child-like trust in Him. The Chinese Christians just believe God and His Word. We believe that He is able and willing to do great things for us."

Speaking further on this very matter of response to the Word, David recounts a visit he made to a remote region of northwestern China, where he preached for about three hours to seventy young people. His theme was "The Lord's Prayer." The listeners were sitting on the floor or leaning against the wall of the little mud hut. They were not just listening, they were writing down every word; and they were weeping.

When David had finished, the house church leader gave him some tea, saying, "After you've had tea you can preach to us again." That was after three hours of solid preaching! He took his tea and then preached for another four or five hours. All the time the young people were taking down notes, and echoing, "Amen! Amen!" Finally, totally exhausted, he sat down.

"Now let us sing," said the leader.

David was shocked as he heard the words of their song: "Don't listen to sermons; don't listen to sermons; we will not listen to sermons . . ."

What kind of response was this to his two sermons lasting seven or eight hours? Then came their real response as they sang from heart and soul, clenching their fists: "We will live out the sermons! We will live out the sermons!"

He went away knowing they would do just that.

The fervent praying and the insatiable appetite for the Word of God that we have recounted in these two chapters simply tell us that these Chinese believers are hungry for God—hungry in a way that we seldom see in the church at large. Their readiness to embrace the cross and to suffer, their determination to witness, their eagerness and fervency in prayer, their love of the fellowship of the saints, their longing for more and more of God's Word, and their whole-hearted response to that Word—all speak of a heart response to God.

Here in the West, we have the same Bible, the same access to God in prayer, the same—or more—opportunity for fellowship, the same Holy Spirit. Why then do we not see this same hunger? Is it not that we have so much to take away our spiritual appetite? Whether we are moving in what are called evangelical, renewal, Pentecostal, or restoration circles, the situation is largely the same. The church has been invaded by a subtle influence that is "not of the Father, but is of the world," and most of us are unaware that we have been affected by it.

In many quarters there has been a strong reaction to certain evangelical anti-worldly teaching of the past. For example, if you were a "zealous Christian" there were "worldly things" you didn't do. It was right to reject that approach as being negative and legalistic. Paul rejected it when he wrote:

> Since you died with Christ to the basic principles of this world, why, as though you still belonged to it, do you submit to its rules: "Do not handle! Do not taste! Do not touch!"? These are all destined to perish with use, because they are based on human commands and teachings.[85]

We saw that one could avoid these things and still be worldly. They were not the true criteria of spirituality. Who could prove from Scripture which of these "evangelical taboos," if any, were wrong? Did we not have liberty to follow our conscience in these areas, without being looked down upon by other Christians?

These were all valid questions, but in a subtle way our view of the world began to change. Of course it had its unacceptable face, but it wasn't really too bad a spot to be in, especially if you were in the "prosperity league" and could afford to live well. With all the exciting new truth about the triumph of the kingdom of God, Scriptures that spoke about our attitude to this world were seldom mentioned:

> My kingdom is not of this world.[86]

> Seek first his kingdom and his righteousness, and all these things [the necessities of life] will be given to you as well.[87]

> Seek the things that are above, where Christ is . . . Set

your minds on things that are above.[88]

Do not love the world or anything in the world. If anyone loves the world, the love of the Father is not in him.[89]

The world and its desires pass away, but the man who does the will of God lives forever.[90]

The thought that as Christians we were "aliens and strangers in the world"[91] and that "our citizenship is in heaven"[92] did not hold any great appeal. We had so much going for us down here. Other-worldliness appeared to be a form of super-spirituality. We did not want anyone thinking we were "too heavenly-minded to be any earthly good." We failed to see that our reaction placed us in a far greater danger of being so earthly-minded we were of no heavenly use!

On top of this there was little or nothing said about the place of the cross in Christian experience, a point we have already made. The cross not only shapes our thinking about sin, about suffering, about the law, but about the world as well. It settles forever what our attitude to the world must be. What Paul said about our not submitting to rules, regulations, and thou-shalt-nots was based on the understanding that we had died to the basic principles of the world. But if we have not embraced the cross our new found "liberty" will never keep the world and its spirit from penetrating our spiritual defenses. Paul himself broke through on this issue, for he wrote:

May I never boast except in the cross of our Lord Jesus Christ, through which the world has been crucified to me, and I to the world.[93]

Christians today, whether evangelical, charismatic, or "restoration," need to be crucified to the world, and the world crucified to them. They are tasting the world, and so have lost their hunger for God. The Chinese church, in contrast, teaches the cross, embraces the cross, dies to the world, lives in heaven—with feet firmly on the earth—and has an insatiable hunger for God.

16

WHERE SUPERNATURAL IS NATURAL

Now, Lord, consider their threats and enable your servants to speak your word with great boldness. Stretch out your hand to heal and perform miraculous signs and wonders through the name of your holy servant Jesus.

Acts 4:29-30

Long before the Communist Revolution, healings and deliverance from demonism had often accompanied work in China. This we have already noticed in connection with the ministry of Pastor Hsi. But during the long dark night of the Cultural Revolution, and the years of rapid church expansion that have followed, supernatural manifestations, especially healings, have become a prominent feature of the movement of the Spirit.

The Acts of the Apostles records many significant thrusts of the Holy Spirit resulting in a harvest of conversions and accelerating the progress of the kingdom. It is significant that every one of these moves of God was precipitated by some supernatural display of His power. As we have been reminded by the words at the head of the chapter, this was what the early Christians asked God to do, and this was exactly what He did in response. Here is another remarkable similarity between the early church and the church in China today.

Speaking of the regular occurrence of healing and miracles in his fellowship, a Christian leader in China said, "Our believers just simply trust the Lord like little children trusting their father. And our heavenly Father cares for and loves us so much He often heals our sick and meets our needs." Or as a Chinese worker, who is constantly in and out of China, put it to me in Hong Kong: "The Christians on the mainland do not consider these things unusual. To them the supernatural has become natural."

Although simplicity of faith is a great quality, unless it is rooted in sound biblical teaching it can lead to superstition and gullibility. Where God is at work, Satan necessarily has his counterfeits. There are many so-called "faith healers," witches, and fortune-tellers in China; and due to lack of teaching, many professing Christians can be gullible and vulnerable. The Communists are very ready to seize upon counterfeits and use them to discredit the real manifestations of the Holy Spirit.

It is obvious that a Communist government will view all healings and miracles as mere superstition. A Christian I heard about who travels regularly behind the Iron Curtain has now been banned from East Germany because of a recent visit when miracles of healing were performed. His traveling companion remarked, "The Communists are terrified of supernatural power." They certainly have reason to be in China. Members of the Communist Party or the People's Liberation Army are not permitted to be Christians. Yet many of these officials are witnessing and experiencing the supernatural power of God, and thus turning to Christ. The repercussions can often be far-reaching.

There is evidence from the Communist authorities themselves that healings are occurring with remarkable frequency throughout the country. The *China Daily*, China's only newspaper in English, put out a report in September 1984 regarding Christian activity in Henan province. It stated that 55 percent of Christians attended worship services because they hoped for healing. The report did not admit that actual healings were taking place, but such a statement would never have been made unless they were. Right from the start, the Three-Self movement, which is required to keep Christianity in line with Party policy, has sought to discredit and discourage any emphasis on healing. This is in keeping with the liberal theology characterizing the top echelon of the movement.

Despite the official attitude, the healing power of God has

constantly been breaking into the ranks of Party members. A special correspondent from Hong Kong records meeting "a number of Party members" in the course of traveling inside China, "some even holding fairly high positions, who had become Christians." There was the Shanghai official whose daughter was healed of leukemia in answer to prayer. This led the father to acknowledge Jesus Christ as Lord and Savior. He is now witnessing for Christ although he has lost his high position, being assigned the job of janitor.

There was also a Party committee secretary suffering from cancer of the esophagus, which, after four months, began to interfere seriously with his eating. The government had given him a substantial sum of money, and the production brigade gave him 500 bricks for funeral preparations as well as a grave site. His wife, who had seen many sick people believe in Jesus and get well, encouraged her husband, "Let us also believe in God."

He replied, "Others may believe, but we cannot. I have persecuted many believers during the Cultural Revolution. Why should God cure me?"

However, his mother-in-law was a Christian, and she pointed out that Jesus did not come for the righteous, but for the sinners. So the Party secretary believed. His mother-in-law then gave him a bowl of soup in Jesus' name and he drank it in faith. Within a few days he was eating normally and recovering rapidly.

While I was in Hong Kong a pastor told me of the case of the Party member who was taken sick. The Communists did not visit him, but the Christians did. They cleaned his house, made meals for him, and took care of him. Their love opened his heart to the reality of Christ and brought him to faith. Then they prayed for him, and God healed him.

In a village in Shaanxi province the Christians were in the middle of a prayer time when the production brigade leader and others burst in upon them. "You are forbidden to believe in Jesus, and you are forbidden to pray," he screeched. Many who were kneeling looked up in alarm, but a few minutes later it was the noisy intruders who had cause for alarm as they looked at their leader. His neck and mouth began to swell terribly and he was gasping for breath. "You must repent and believe in Christ," said the Christians. The man nodded his assent, began to pray, and immediately the swelling went down, and he began to praise God out loud.

So the production leader was changed from a persecutor of Christians to a dedicated disciple of Christ. Now he witnesses wherever he goes, and has already led many people to Christ. The church was not only protected but has been able to expand its ministry.

A young man in the People's Liberation Army was a sincere believer, although this is forbidden. When one of his fellows was taken seriously ill, the Christian became deeply concerned that the man would die without Christ and so shared the gospel with him. The man's condition continued to deteriorate; but he took his friend's advice, turned to Christ, and was almost instantly healed.

When his superiors found out, they tried to reeducate him in various ways, but he refused to give up his faith. His experience of healing had brought the awe of God upon him. The authorities concluded that they could do nothing with him, so they threw him out of the army. This would affect his education and employment for the rest of his life, but he was too amazed at how the Lord had healed him to do anything else but believe. "Today," concludes a report, "he serves the Lord with that sense of awe."

A Christian wife on mainland China had been in ill health for some time, finally developing pains in the liver. She kept on losing weight; the pain became unbearable. The doctor's verdict was cancer of the liver, for which he could do nothing. The Christian husband was in a state of depression when a letter came from Asian Outreach in Hong Kong. In the letter was a quotation from Ephesians 3. As the husband read the passage, these words lit up with a bright light: "able to do immeasurably more than all we ask or imagine."

Convinced that the disease was incurable, he had only been asking God to reduce the pain. "I did not ask God to heal her. I dared not ask, I dared not hope." He read the verses to the family and from then on they prayed every morning for God's healing. Within five days the pain stopped. His wife began to put on weight as though she was "a balloon being inflated." The doctor thought she was "bloated," but found her muscles firm and strong. The family told the doctor that God had healed her. Though still weak at the time of the report, she was able to take care of her family and was confident that she would be fully restored.

The New Testament distinguishes between healings and miracles.[94] Like the one just recounted, many of these healings were in response to a prayer of faith, and had not been instantaneous. The promise of Jesus is, "They will place their hands on sick people, and they will get well."[95] This may or may not be instantaneous. Of course miracles are not confined to miracles of healing. When is a healing a miracle? When it is both instantaneous and manifest to all who behold. When people exclaim "Wow!" then that is a miracle. There have been many instances where God's supernatural working has brought forth the "Wow!" of wonder from the lips of those who witnessed it.

This story goes back to the early days of the Cultural Revolution. It is recounted by a young man whose family came from the hated landlord class, and who was healed before he knew the Lord. He described those terrible days for his family, while they waited for the inevitable: "Since there was nowhere to flee we waited for death at home." Tragedy hit his family in 1967 when the dormitory where he was living was struck by lightning. It set his clothes and hair on fire, and his body was seriously burned. People who came to put out the fire ignored him. Their only concern was to rescue the picture of Mao, and his works. His mother, some distance away in the female dormitory, was lifted out of bed as though compelled by some strange force. She rushed to his dormitory. Pushing aside the fireman, she threw herself into the flames and rescued him.

Two days later he recovered consciousness in the hospital. He was too weak even to lift a finger, and the burns on his body were festering, but the doctor told his mother, "Your unit requires you to return and be reformed through labor. The boy cannot stay in the hospital." He also told her that because of the burns the nervous system was seriously damaged, and that he would be handicapped for life. Without a word his mother put him on a wooden cart and wheeled him home.

Three months later, while his mother was at work, a golden light flooded the room where the boy was lying, and he found he could sit up. The light seemed to be coming in from the mountainside, filling the whole cottage. He moved to get out of bed. As his feet touched the floor he felt a warm current of "electricity" running through his hands and feet. On her return, his mother was struck dumb with astonishment to see him walking about. "Heaven has eyes," she said. In 1969, when amid the tears of the family he was sent to the countryside, his mother said to him, "Child, go! Don't come back. You are different from the others. You are heaven-born and heaven-raised."

He searched earnestly for God, and tried in vain to get hold of a Bible. Eventually God brought him to Hong Kong. There he was put in touch with the Chinese Church Research Center where he found Christ. Here is his testimony:

> I firmly believe that God chose me to be a part of His people even before I was born. I am grateful to God for His enlightenment, His gifts, and His selection. I thank God for His guidance one step at a time, for carrying me into His presence, and embracing me in His bosom at the right time. Because of Him I have experienced a Spirit-filled baptism and am experiencing abundant Christian life.

Asian Outreach workers delivered a Bible to a young medical doctor in a small town of central China. He recounted how a peasant woman who had had a very bad accident was brought into the hospital. A rock had crushed her chest, her rib cage was broken, and some of her ribs had pierced her lungs. There was little he could do to save her life. As he placed the semi-conscious woman back on her bed, he heard her pray, "Jesus, help me!"

Next day he was totally astonished to find the woman sitting up in bed eating a bowl of rice gruel. He had her X-rayed again, and was even more astonished to find that every single piece of her rib cage was perfectly healed! He told us, "I have now personally seen the power of Jesus." This man had never before seen a Bible or the inside of a church, but he was a firm believer in Christ.

There have also been cases of God's miraculous

provision.   A home in a Chinese village held a special
meeting to which many people traveled long distances.   On
their arrival the lady of the house served a hot meal, with
food which the travelers had brought with them.   Later on
another group arrived.   The lady knew they would be
hungry, but she had no food left.   She went into the kitchen to
see what she could find.   There were pots with meat and
vegetables in them.   Supposing that the new arrivals had
brought their own food, she served it up, and afterwards
thanked them for bringing the food.   "What food?" they
asked.   "We didn't bring any food.   We ate all our provisions
along the way."   They had experienced a mini-miracle of the
"five loaves and two small fishes" type.

The authority Christ gives His people to deal with
demonism is still a great door-opener for the gospel in China.
Here is a recent testimony of a forty-five-year-old mother of
four boys, whose husband was an engineer.   They lived in
Qinghai, a sparsely populated province next to Tibet.   After
two boys, she wanted a girl, and prayed to Buddha that this
third child she was carrying would be a daughter.   To her
great disappointment she had another boy.   When this
happened a fourth time she felt tricked, and lost control of
herself.   She left the baby on the ground to freeze to death,
but her husband rescued him.

She became desperate when her husband was sent away
to take a course, and the devil seemed to take over.   She
wanted neither her husband nor her children, she just
wanted to die.   Once she tried to hang herself, but was
discovered just in time.   Her husband was recalled.   He tried
many famous doctors, all to no avail.   His wife was like a
mad woman.   He decided to move his family back to
Shandong.

By 1981 the husband and the four boys were caring for
the demented woman all the time and all family joy had
gone.   He sought help from witches, and these cost him a lot
of money.   Early in 1983 a witch prophesied that his wife
would get better at the time of the Spring Festival.   The event
came and went, and there was no improvement.   The witch
then admitted, "My god is no longer effective.   You had better
try Jesus!"   Previously some Christians had urged him to

trust in Jesus, but he had not heeded. But now, in desperation, he was ready to heed the witch's advice.

Hearing of a meeting in the village, the husband, helped by his sons, balanced his wife on a bicycle and wheeled her there. On the way she tried to throw herself into a well, screaming, "After six years I can't bear any more!" The Christians were having Sunday worship. When they saw her they united in prayer, and the demon was eventually cast out. Now they are a Christian family. The wife testified, "From then on I have never missed a meeting ... My home is now full of joy as Jesus is the head of our household."

There have been prophetic words of warning given to Christians in times of danger. Three hundred pastors from different cities and towns had come together for a three-day meeting. The authorities found out about it and sent secret police to investigate. As the pastors were praying, the word of the Lord came to one of them: "The situation here is very dangerous. The police are coming to arrest you." One by one the pastors dispersed, using different routes.

As soon as the last one was gone, the police came and the building was surrounded. They waited for the pastors to leave so that they could arrest them. Eventually they became impatient and were ready to break down the door. To their surprise they found it ajar and the room empty. The leader exclaimed in amazement more than in anger, "These Christians are different. They know exactly what we are doing."

In 1981 Christians in a certain city in Zhejiang province persuaded a printing company to print 10,000 copies of *Streams in the Desert*,[96] a favorite devotional book in China. The firm did not realize that permission always has to be obtained from the authorities. When they found out, the printing was already completed; they only needed to cut the paper and bind the books. The police told them the books would be destroyed. Hearing this, the Christians began moving the materials from the factory to their homes to complete the project themselves.

Only a few books were left when the police, learning what was happening, set a trap. They sent the army to surround the factory, waiting for the Christians to come that night so that they could arrest them. But the Lord spoke to the believers and told them to stay away. The soldiers waited all night, and next morning left before replacements arrived. At that very point the believers came and took the rest of the books away.

On finding there was not a single book left as evidence, the police were furious. They arrested the manager, fined him heavily, and put him in prison for ten days. When the believers visited him, he said, "Do not feel bad. It is worth going to prison for ten days if one can get the message out. I will do it any time!" The incident was publicized as a news item: "Printing company accepts order for illegal propaganda material."

These incidents are a small sample of the wonderful things God is doing in China. The full story will probably never be told. I have reserved for the following chapter part of the story of the remarkable way in which angelic ministry has been used to serve the body of Christ. Angels have been used not only in deliverance and protection, but even in miracles of healing. It seems to fit in completely with the spontaneous nature of the Spirit's working in that land.

17

HEAVEN'S AGENTS

Are not all angels ministering spirits sent to serve those who will inherit salvation?

Hebrews 1:14

Angels are continually around us. We are often the unconscious recipients of their watchful care. As the messengers of God's presence, they may bring words of comfort, hope, or counsel, often in situations of crisis or at a strategic point in God's dealing with men. It is at such times that we become conscious of their presence, as they break through that thin veil that separates the visible from the invisible.

The early Christians were strong believers in the ministry of angels. When Peter stood knocking at the door of the home where Christians were praying for his release from prison, a young woman named Rhoda went to answer the knock. She recognized Peter's voice and ran back to tell the praying saints that they could get off their knees—the answer to their prayers was knocking at the door. "You're out of your mind," they told her. "It must be his angel."[97] They weren't so far from the mark. His angel had only left him a short while before, after getting him outside the prison gate!

As the conflict of the end time intensifies, and as persecution becomes the order of the day, we may expect to hear much more about angelic protection and provision. We have a lot to learn about this neglected theme. Perhaps it is because the situation in China is in so many ways similar to New Testament times that angelic visitations are not uncommon there.

During the Cultural Revolution a pastor in the far north of China was sentenced to public execution by firing squad because he refused to quit preaching the gospel. While the squad was getting ready he was asked if he had any last request. He replied that he would like to sing a song. Since it was a public execution permission was granted. He sang out in a booming voice, and as he sang the sky began to light up with the splendor of God's glory. All the people who were gathered around heard what sounded like thousands of voices singing along with the pastor.

Shaken by the incident, the authorities decided to postpone the execution while an urgent telegram was sent off to Beijing for advice. Because of its nature the telegram quickly found its way up the bureaucratic ladder until it reached Premier Zhou Enlai. Informed of the matter in detail, he sent back communication: "This truly is no ordinary man. Release him and don't even bother him again." The pastor was speedily released to do whatever he wanted, and he immediately began preaching. As far as is known he is still doing that today. Part of the song he sang, translated into English, reads:

Lord, I love you!
My heart seeks after you.
Because of you I forsake everything,
And despise wealth and fame.

Paul Kauffman tells of a young Christian sent from his home town to work in a commune hundreds of miles away on the island of Hainan. Because of his isolation he had become lukewarm in his faith. One night when he was asleep in the dormitory with his fellow workers a typhoon hit the island. Such storms, bringing gales of up to 100 miles per hour, are not uncommon there.

In the midst of the howling storm the young man was startled by someone calling his name outside the dormitory. He sat up in bed, but was reluctant to go out because of the danger. Finally, the voice was so insistent that he went out.

At that moment the building collapsed behind him. Several were killed and all were injured. As a result of this experience, the young man found a boldness in witnessing that he had never had before. More than 200 people came to Christ in the following eighteen months.[98]

In 1975 there was a church that held retreats and training classes for young converts in the nearby mountains. They were having a baptismal service for 100 converts when militia men arrived to prevent the baptisms. However, they saw soldiers surrounding the Christians, and so withdrew their detachment in the belief that the army had the matter in hand. The only soldiers were from the heavenly army, so the baptismal service proceeded without interference.

In conversation with representatives of Open Doors, Brother Nui of China was asked what the Christians did at their Sunday evening meetings since there were few Bibles, fewer songbooks, and no Bible teacher. He said that they came together to praise God for what He had done, and then would give several testimonies of the wonderful things that God was doing.

Among the events he recounted was that of a small boy who went out with his grandmother to the fields. He was killed when he was run over by a heavily loaded cart. The grandmother was overwhelmed with fear and buried the boy herself. Afraid to tell her daughter what had happened, she said that the child had wandered off in the streets. The grief-stricken family was having dinner when the little boy walked into the home. He explained that a man in white had lifted him from the ground, brushed off the dirt from his clothes and face, and told him to go back home.

Mr. Huang was a Buddha-worshiper. His health began to deteriorate until he could not keep any food down. The doctor diagnosed cancer of the liver in the terminal stage, and said there was nothing that could be done for him, so he returned to his native village to await death. While there he heard about a doctor in the town and decided to get a second opinion. This doctor, who was a Christian (and accompanied the man as he gave this testimony), confirmed that the diagnosis was correct and that the illness was incurable.

He then told the man that there was no medicine that could prolong his life, but that if he would believe in Jesus Christ, he could have eternal life. The gospel was explained to him and he was urged to believe on the Lord Jesus Christ. The doctor also explained that Jesus had the power to heal any sickness, if that was His will.

"But whether Jesus heals you or not is not important," said the doctor. "What is important is that you have eternal life."

Mr. Huang said, "I want to believe in Jesus." They knelt in the doctor's office as Mr. Huang became a new person in Christ.

On his return home he told his wife of his faith in Christ and asked her to remove all the idols from the house and burn them. She did this, but Mr. Huang's condition deteriorated rapidly. Every night he and his wife knelt to pray. He thanked the Lord that whatever happened to him physically, he now had eternal life. He was gripped by terrible pain, and became so weak that the family began preparations for his funeral. The coffin was purchased and the grave dug on the hillside.

One night a man in a white robe appeared to him in his sleep. He was holding a knife. Fearing his intentions, Mr. Huang struggled with him, but the man prevailed and touched Mr. Huang with the knife. Next morning he awoke at eight o'clock, hungry for the first time in many days. After eating a nourishing bowl of soup he fell asleep.

When he awoke he saw clearly two men in white robes standing by his bed. They said, "You have been healed." He reached down and found all of his swelling gone. Being extremely hungry, he ate a hearty meal. When his brother came to pay him a visit, he was amazed to see him sitting up. He testified to his brother that Jesus had touched him during the night and he was completely healed.

From Zhejiang, a province reputed to have a very large number of Christians, comes this story of a village woman with a brain tumor. For nine years she had tried to find a cure, spending all her money in vain. She then gave up all hope and resigned herself to die.

One day, lying on her bed alone in the house, she saw

three people in white robes enter her room. One of them asked her, "Do you want to be healed?"

A little surprised, she replied, "Are you a doctor? Yes, I want to be healed."

The man in white came near and stroked her head where the tumor was. She felt fluid coming out of her head and a lump being removed. The man then seemed to close up the opening with a few quick movements of his fingers. She felt instantly relieved. Then she asked, "What is your name, doctor?"

"Jesus," the man in white answered. "You may find Me in the nearest town." Then He disappeared.

When the family returned in the evening she told them about the doctor who gave her free treatment. They paid no attention to her, thinking she was delirious. But she grew stronger every day; her brain tumor was gone. Then she set out for the neighboring town to find the doctor who had healed her, in order to thank him.

"Is there a doctor here by the name of Jesus?" The woman she addressed was a Christian, who thought for a second, and then decided to take the enquirer to her home where Christians gathered to worship. She told her story. The Christians were not surprised to hear of her healing as it is so common in rural China. But she was awestruck when they told her who Jesus was. They preached repentance and salvation to her and she went home with Jesus in her heart.

Shortly afterward her whole family came to Christ. Her testimony quickly spread in her village, and many people wanted to believe in Jesus. She brought in a more mature Christian from the neighboring town to help out. As a result of her healing many people came to the Lord.

A very poor Christian couple made their living hauling stones and logs on wooden handcarts. They were straining to get a heavy load of stones up a hill. When they reached the top, the wife ran around to the front to steady the cart on the reverse slope. She tripped and fell, and the cart passed over her body, crushing her bones. Local doctors said she would have to go to a larger hospital for major surgery, but this was far more than the couple could afford.

On the fourth night in the hospital the drugs were still

giving her no relief from her extreme pain. As she waited on the Lord, she decided to stop all the painkillers and trust God for healing. That night two "strangers" visited her. They lifted her by the shoulders and pressed down on her pelvic bone. She said it was as though "boiling water" was passing through her body from head to foot. When she awoke the next morning she kept saying, "Thank you, Lord! Praise the Lord!"

"What's the matter?" asked the lady in the next bed.

"My body is well again," she replied. "The angels have operated on my bones."

When the doctors came to examine her, she told them what had happened. They were amazed to find that her bones were perfect. She was allowed to check out of the hospital at noon that day.

A few days later she went to the market and bought some fruit and candies. Then she stood by the road and stopped people as they passed to tell them her testimony of God's healing power. To each who would listen, she gave some fruit and candy—her thank offering![99]

For several generations Dr. Wang's family had lived in a two-story house surrounding a local courtyard. Despite misgivings at the time of the Communist Revolution, he had worked hard to serve the people. When the Cultural Revolution struck, old Dr. Wang, trained in Western medicine and known to be a Christian, was one of the first targets for persecution. No one quite knows what they did to him, for he never spoke about his sufferings; but Dr. Wang could no longer walk. He was confined to his bed in an upstairs room, and was cared for by his family.

One night, as Dr. Wang's daughter-in-law lay awake, unable to sleep, she heard the creaking sound of the great wooden gate into the courtyard. Springing up, she ran to the narrow veranda to see a white-clad figure enter the house. She went downstairs to investigate, but no one was there, except family members fast asleep.

Meanwhile, in the little room upstairs, Dr. Wang stirred in his sleep. A bright light shone down upon him; his eyes opened to a vision of the Lord Jesus standing beside the bed. "Son," he heard Jesus say. "Get up and walk!"

"I cannot walk," he replied with surprise. So Jesus reached out His hands and lifted him up.

"Do you believe in Me?" Jesus asked.

"I do, I do, Lord!" he answered.

"If you believe in Me," Jesus said, "get up and walk."

Without hesitation the old man obeyed. He rose from his bed and began walking. Then he began to laugh out loud with joy, and it seemed that the Lord laughed with him. It was two-thirty in the morning. The laughter woke his nephew who slept in the same room. He thought his uncle had gone out of his mind, and rushed to support him lest he fall.

In another room, Dr. Wang's eldest son was awakened by the commotion. He jumped up and was shocked to see his father standing by his bed, laughing. He too thought the old man had gone mad. He was about to clutch him when his father said very firmly, "Keep your hands off me! I am not out of my mind. The Lord Jesus came to this room! He has healed me!" With these words he walked down the steep stairway to the first floor, turned around, and smiled up at his frightened family. Then he began walking up again with steady steps. As he reached the top, the joy of the family knew no bounds. Their excitement woke up everyone in the household.

Such good news could not wait until morning. The entire family trooped over to the second son's home in another street. "Look! Grandpa is walking!" cried the youngest son, as one by one the startled family members joined the excited group. Laughing and rejoicing, they gave thanks to God together.

Dr. Wang wanted to go on to the meeting place of the believers, but his sons persuaded him to wait until morning. At dawn the family went to the astonished pastor and then to other relatives. They met Dr. Wang's young niece on her way to work. She stared open-mouthed to see him walking. On hearing what had happened she began to praise the Lord, saying, "Blessed be our God! He is so wonderful!"

The following Sunday, the house where the believers gathered for worship was crowded out. People stood in the courtyard and looked in through the windows. Others filled the alleyway. All eyes were on old Dr. Wang, who was moving from room to room greeting the Christians. He told his amazing story to a hushed company. Afterward, questions flew.

"Dr. Wang, can you jump?" asked the pastor.

"Can I jump? Of course I can!" said the old man, and with that he began to jump up and down for all to see.

Dr. Wang now travels far and wide on his bicycle telling all who will listen about the power of Jesus. People are not only listening, they are calling upon the name of the Lord and being saved.

Many will want to know if these independent house churches in China are "charismatic." That really depends on what you mean by the term. If you are asking, "Are these Christians open to the in-filling and gifts of the Holy Spirit? Do they expect God to do today what He did in Bible times? Do they view such things as normal when they do occur?" the answer would almost certainly be "yes" to all these questions. When it comes to healing there is surely more faith among the house churches of China than there is among the majority of believers in the West who call themselves "pentecostal" or "charismatic."

If, however, you mean, "Is there clear teaching on the baptism in the Holy Spirit and the spiritual gifts? Is there real freedom in praise and worship? Does the exercise of tongues, interpretation of tongues, and prophecy feature in their meetings?" the answer would largely be "no." Of course I am generalizing, and there will be numerous exceptions to these two answers.

Chinese Christians almost universally accept the fact that God heals today. They believe in the validity of the gifts and manifestations of the Spirit, and are open to them; but there's probably little emphasis on earnestly desiring them, as Paul exhorts us to do, and little biblical teaching on their proper exercise in the church.

What does God want to say to us through this aspect of His work in China? In a nation which is largely free from the influence of the West, and where there is no strong "lobby" for or against supernatural manifestations, God is nonetheless moving spontaneously in this way. What does that say to us? The reason healings feature so prominently in this move of God is surely that they are so mightily effective in this current phase of evangelistic growth. Do we not desperately need such growth in our own land?

The other lesson is the openness of the Chinese believers and the simplicity of their faith. It is true that they have had little teaching. In the mercy of God, no one has been around to warn them that "these things" were "confined to early Christianity," and that "God does not work in these ways today," and that therefore any such manifestations are "counterfeit." Thus when God began to work in such ways they welcomed such working with great gladness.

We need to come out of our pose of negativism or neutrality, if we have adopted such. We need to begin to call on the Lord, as the early church did, and as the church in China is now doing, asking that He would stretch forth His hand to heal and that signs and wonders may be done.

A time must surely come in China when this present phase of phenomenal growth gives way to one of consolidation. Then I believe God will lead those churches to seek the gifts that are specially given for edification. Scriptures will be illuminated for them, such as: "... Eagerly desire ... spiritual gifts, especially the gift of prophecy";[100] and, "Since you are eager to have spiritual gifts, try to excel in gifts that build up the church."[101] Not only gifts of teaching and exhortation, but also the public use of tongues in conjunction with interpretation, the gift of prophecy, and others come into this category.[102] One thing is certain: God will not withhold any good gift that is needed for the maturing of His church in China.

18

HOUSE CHURCHES EAST AND WEST

You too are being built together to become a dwelling in which God lives by his spirit.

Ephesians 2:22

In their human origins there is no apparent connection between the house churches in China and New Testament churches that have sprung up in the West as well as in other parts of the world. That makes their similarities, which we are now to consider, all the more significant. A builder friend of mine put his house, which he built himself, on the market. He could tell that the man who came to view it was in the construction business by the things he spotted and the remarks he made. When this prospective purchaser came for a second look, he said, "I can pick out your houses all over town." It was not that they were all the same, but that they had distinctive features. There is great variety and flexibility in New Testament churches, but there are also distinctive features that tell us that the "architect and builder is God."

There is always a timing for God's working. This provides an interesting connection between East and West. It may not be possible to pinpoint the beginnings of the house churches in China as we now know them, for there were cottage meetings before the Communists took over, and homes were used in the early years of their regime. The "birth" or breaking out of the movement came with the end of the Cultural Revolution. So the germination was taking place during those dark days (1966-1978) when the Christian church was underground.

It was at this very time that God began to move hearts in Britain with a great longing for the restoration of New Testament Christianity. Conferences were held, hearts were stirred, and in 1972 there was a knitting together of a handful of leaders who shared the same vision. Here were the beginnings of a restoration movement that has brought forth hundreds of new churches. In the early days many of these met in homes, so they became known as the "house church movement." But as growth compelled them to move into larger premises, and at the same time many traditional churches began to develop mid-week home groups, the term "house church" became something of a misnomer. The movement in Britain now embraces many streams and numerous individual churches not organizationally connected.

God told that first group of men in England that they were not to think themselves above their brothers in any way because of what He was showing them. They were only an example; what God was doing with them He would do with others all over the world. They had no idea that He was including Christians in China. They discovered about two years later that God had moved similarly and at about the same time with a group of men in the U.S. Since then, other individuals and groups whose hearts were similarly stirred by the Holy Spirit, and who had found a new relationship, have come to light. The timings of God are significant.

In comparing East with West it is immediately apparent that the way God worked in China to bring to birth the kind of churches He wanted was utterly different than in, say, Britain or the U.S. In China it was mainly through the iron fist of communism and the pressure of circumstances; here in the West, it was more by revelation and conviction—but the same Architect and Builder was at work in each situation.

The first comparison concerns a return to simplicity. God used the Communists, as we have seen, to break down the denominational structures of the churches in China. Their idea was to force believers into the common mold of the

Three-Self Patriotic Movement. Many Christians refused to be so forced. Families began to meet in their homes for prayer and Bible study. Others began to find one another in new relationships. The old Western denominational wineskin was gone, although much of the old form was being resurrected in the Three-Self movement.

Like the churches of the New Testament, the only structure these persecuted believers now had was one of great simplicity. This structure is built when heart is knitted to heart and unity is formed by the action of the Holy Spirit. They discovered that this kind of joining together *is* the house of God, the place where God is pleased to dwell by His Spirit.

For us in the West it was a simplicity that we began to see and to hunger for. This simplicity did not just happen. We did not discover it; God revealed it to our seeking hearts. Though we did not have to endure beatings and imprisonment, that does not mean that obedience to the heavenly vision was without price. It nearly always brings on misunderstanding, criticism, and reproach.

Second, anointed leadership was brought forth. Slowly but surely the Communists increased their stranglehold on the church. If leaders did not readily cooperate by joining the official church, they were subjected to "struggle sessions" and every other conceivable kind of
Some cracked; others found themselves sentenced to many years in prison. Meanwhile, God was quietly at work in many home groups, preparing and training a new generation of leaders for a new day that was to dawn.

Outside the Three-Self movement there was now no denominational hierarchy—no synods, boards, or councils to choose and appoint new leaders. These institutions were being eliminated by circumstances, just as they were in the early church. It was not difficult for the mature saints to recognize those on whom the Spirit's anointing rested. A man's qualification for ministry was not that he had been selected by a board or had a diploma from some seminary, but that he knew God and had been chosen, called, and gifted by God for the job he was doing.

It may not be possible at this stage to identify all the gifts that God is bestowing on His people in China. Much is still in the formative stage. But this much is clear: He is raising up many teachers, pastors, evangelists, and those used in healing. In answer to prayer, He will surely provide all that His church needs for its future development.

This is the basis on which leadership is recognized in the many churches with which I am familiar in the West. There are people with apostolic and prophetic gifts whom God uses to spot, train, and encourage emerging leaders. I do not know whether that is yet happening in China. Certainly in the past China has produced men of apostolic gift. But the indispensable qualification for leadership, East or West, is knowing God and having the anointing of His Spirit.

The third area is congregational participation. Paul wrote to the Corinthians: "When you come together, everyone has a hymn, or a word of instruction, or a revelation . . ."[103] This way of proceeding does not go well with the formal church setting, but is a natural way of operating in a family setting, and in church the Chinese Christians have rediscovered "family." The many-membered body has found itself, and its members are functioning. This was one of the open secrets of the rapid development and maturing of the believers in New Testament times. The same process is now taking place in China.

Back in the West we have come to recognize the importance of this principle out of our understanding of "the body of Christ," and because God has bestowed upon the body the gifts of the Holy Spirit. Such participation is often called "body ministry." What is the point of "the manifestation of the Spirit" being given to each one in the body,[104] if only the man at the front is really free to exercise his gift? How quickly the believers develop and mature when they learn to step out in faith and participate by giving thanks, praying, testifying, or exercising a spiritual gift. A body functioning in this way is also fertile ground for raising up new leadership.

In the previous two chapters I have spoken of the Chinese Christians' openness to the Holy Spirit and to His supernatural manifestations. For this reason one would expect them to be at home in those churches in the West where such gifts and manifestations are free to operate, but not so comfortable in churches that insist such things are not for today. I recall a visit to northern Thailand years ago. Many among the hill tribes had found Christ, and churches had been established. A serious rift had occurred between these believers and the missionary organization working in the area because of the mission policy of discouraging any manifestations of the Spirit. The native believers could not understand the missionaries' attitude toward something that was so clearly scriptural and that had brought them such blessing.

Circumstances, providentially, have prevented the Chinese believers from thinking in terms of "consecrated buildings." We have seen that they meet in private homes, warehouses, even in business premises, courtyards, or in the open air. Very occasionally, in rural areas, they may be able to secure a building for worship. But often they are compelled to move from home to home. This has been a continual reminder that the church is not the building, and the "sanctuary" is not the bricks and mortar. As the old hymn put it—

> Where e'er they seek thee thou art found,
> And every place is hallowed ground.

This view also shapes the thinking of the New Testament churches in the West. They are not against the procuring of buildings as meeting places, but they believe that the expenditure of vast sums of money on church property is not only a misapplication of the resources entrusted to them, but is a serious hindrance to swift growth as well. Elaborate and costly buildings put the emphasis on the wrong thing. This kind of expenditure does not seem to take into account the end-time shaking predicted in Scripture.[105] What would happen to such buildings in a time of prolonged persecution? The fact that the Communists have taken over missionary schools, hospitals, and church buildings for secular purposes must make us wonder whether the large sums involved could have been more wisely spent.

Finally, these churches in East and West have a similar attitude to spiritual mixture in the professing church. The

Chinese do not have to cope with quite the same denominational hodgepodge that we face in the West. In China it is all in one bag—the Three-Self Patriotic Movement. The house church leaders know that the Religious Affairs Bureau of the Communist government, which is entirely political, calls the tune, and the official church has to comply. To most house church leaders this involves denying the lordship of Christ over His church, and though they acknowledge that there are good men in the Three-Self movement, they will not join, for that would be compromise.

Many church leaders outside China, even evangelicals, have been beguiled by the smooth words of Bishop Ding and his colleagues, who head up the Three-Self movement and its sister organization, the China Christian Council. They travel overseas, trying to convince the outside world that China has human rights and religious freedom. This is a travesty of truth when you know that pastors from the house churches are still being arrested, their churches closed, and their flocks told that they must now worship in the newly opened Three-Self churches. "There is no religious freedom," says Paul Kauffman. "Communism cannot permit freedom. It can and does permit some practice of religion. This is a very important distinction. All religion is carefully controlled by the State." Christians are told where they are to worship, who is allowed to preach, the parish to which he is confined, and what may be printed and published.

No Bibles or Christian literature may be printed without permission of the Religious Affairs Bureau. Young people do not have religious freedom. It is an offense to try to influence them with the gospel. Three-Self Bibles in the past have been in the traditional script, which is no longer taught in the schools. The authorities do not want young people to read and believe. These are some of the reasons why so many of the leaders of the unofficial churches take a strong stand, refusing to compromise with the official church, though in towns and cities they are under increasing pressure to do so.

In the West, though the situation is completely different, New Testament-type churches generally take a radical stance on denominational mixture. This may have caused some churches to develop an exclusive posture, but most have warm relationships with those in traditional and independent church settings. However, they do not allow these relationships to weaken their convictions with regard to New Testament principles they have embraced. They do not want to belong to an "official church," whatever the immediate advantages may appear to be, any more than do their brothers and sisters in China. Their convictions about the church make them radical.

We have looked at seven significant characteristics of house churches, East and West. But how important are they? Ours is a practical God, as well as a God of principle. When we adopt New Testament ways we are also being pragmatic. God's ways work best. He has taken every contingency into consideration.

Let us look at two aspects of the practical importance of these characteristics. First, denominational Christianity, with its central organization and complex machinery, is brittle rather than flexible; and where the civil authority is antagonistic, it is easily brought under government control—as in China. It can then be weakened, and, when it has served its purpose, destroyed. That is the Communist theory. The New Testament church structure is simple and flexible, designed to survive and even flourish in times of persecution.

"The more imposing the edifice, the more easily it is found by the gunner. The more obvious and obtrusive an organization, the more readily it is attacked and ruined."[106] We can see the significance of this principle in China, but we are very foolish and shortsighted if we suppose that this situation could never overtake us in the West. As I have said before, the predictions of Scripture are clear. As the end-time conflict intensifies, persecution will become much more widespread. "He is worst prepared who is least prepared for the worst."

Second, the simplicity of New Testament churches means that they are geared for mission and for growth. The Chinese house churches have been divested of surplus baggage. Their resources are channeled into evangelism and shepherding. Their understanding of community gives them a sense of belonging and of cohesion. Their emphasis on the "body" encourages everyone to participate. Nonfunctioning members are a small minority. Each feels he has a part to play, so there is a high deployment of the church's potential.

It must be admitted that in the early years of the house church movement in Britain much of the growth came through discontented believers who found in the new churches the kind of fellowship they were looking for. This has brought from some disgruntled pastors the rather foolish charge of "sheep stealing." The two-legged variety are not stolen! If they move, they move of their own volition. I have yet to come across any church that turns away hungry sheep looking for fresh grass and still waters.

Now the situation is rapidly changing. New churches everywhere are mobilizing for evangelism, and a growing proportion of their numerical increase is from new converts with no church background. One wishes they were all like that—they are so much easier to shepherd! We are now in a situation where it is New Testament churches, whether East or West, with a structure geared for mission, that are by and large the fastest growing churches of the twentieth century.

19

A CRY FOR HELP

*He has delivered us from such a deadly
peril, and he will deliver us. On him we
have set our hope that he will continue
to deliver us, as you help us by your
prayers.*

2 Corinthians 1:10-11

As I have been writing, my mind has traveled back to my
first visit to New Zealand in 1963. A number had been
stirred at that time to pray for the outpouring of the Holy
Spirit. In Auckland I met some godly women who were true
intercessors. "Has God shown you anything about China?"
one of them asked me.

"No," I replied.

"Well, He has shown us," came the reply, "that that great
land, now so tightly closed, will one day open right up to the
gospel—and we are praying for that to happen." At that
point China's darkest hour, the Cultural Revolution, was
still in the future. But God heard the prayers of many saints
throughout the world, and delivered His people "from such a
deadly peril."

In 1975 China was again approaching a crucial era, one
destined to set the whole nation on a new course. A
worldwide prayer movement was set in motion, finding
expression in Britain during the following two years in the
"China—too hard for God?" campaign. This set hundreds of
British Christians praying. The year 1976 witnessed the
death of Mao Zedong as well as the arrest and imprisonment
of the Gang of Four, who had planned to seize power and
keep the country on a leftist course. The more liberal policies

that followed opened the way for a great movement of the Spirit. The hopes of the Chinese Christians that God would "continue to deliver" were fulfilled through the help of many prayers.

There are numerous ways in which we can play a part in what God is now doing in China: taking in Bibles and Christian literature; supporting ministries into China, especially radio broadcasts; befriending Chinese students in our universities, with a view to witnessing to them; and so on. But this chapter will try to give some guidelines on the question of prayer help, as that is part of God's commission in the writing of this book.

There has been much publicity about the shortage of Bibles and Christian literature, especially in the rural areas. Although it is most important that we pray and support those who are seeking to meet this need, an even greater need is that of anointed leadership. The church of the first century grew and flourished without the general availability of Scriptures, but this could not have happened without leadership. The need for Bibles and literature is being met, although there is much more to be done, but the immediate need can be relieved with the raising up of mature leadership.

We need to pray for the ministries of apostles, prophets, evangelists, pastors, and teachers,[107] which Paul reminds us are the gifts of the ascended Christ to His body. China has had men of apostolic caliber in the past, like Pastor Hsi and Watchman Nee, who have been true church planters. But they are needed more than ever today to shape and structure the Chinese church of the future. There is also a need for prophets, men with prophetic vision and insight who will help guide the church through the difficult days that lie ahead.

God is already raising up evangelists, shepherds, and teachers, but the need for them is still great. As an elderly pastor put it, "Before the Communists came, I remember that shepherds were searching for sheep. But now, all over China, it is the sheep who are searching for shepherds!" These gifts are bestowed in response to prayer. The answer lies within the scope and ministry of the intercessor.

In reading these pages, have we heard God speak to us through the church in China? Have we recognized that this is a current word for us? The church in China, as are God's people everywhere, is prophetic; that is, they have a "now" word for their day and generation. We need to pray that they may come into a fuller understanding of their destiny in God and their prophetic calling, not only to Communist China but to the whole world.

When God first spoke to me about writing this book, and then opened the way for me to visit China, I prayed that He would give me a traveling companion, preferably Chinese but at least fluent in Mandarin, who would take me in and provide the openings. I had hoped for introductions to house church leaders, and hoped perhaps to see for myself a house church in action. God did not fulfill these desires, at least not on that first trip. Instead it proved to be the loneliest trip I have ever made in thirty-five years of itinerant ministry.

I had flown into Shanghai, where I hoped to be joined by an American brother and a party of Chinese from Hong Kong. My American friend at first failed to locate me. In the guest house where I was staying I dined in solitary grandeur. The authorities were at that time careful to ensure that foreign visitors had as little contact as possible with the Chinese.

I will never forget taking a taxi to a department store in the heart of Shanghai. It was a few days before the Chinese New Year. I found myself literally propelled into the store by the shoving, milling crowd. It was just like being at Times Square on New Year's Eve. I had never seen such crowds. Back on the streets, I could not communicate. I looked in vain for a Western face. During that hour a thousand pairs of Chinese eyes must have surveyed me with curiosity. Surely some of these people must be Christians, I thought. I had been told there were one million in Shanghai. A great longing swept over me just to grip one believer's hand, just to exchange a smile of greeting, just to say that word that every Christian knows, whatever his language—"Hallelujah." But there was no way we could find each other. I had never experienced such a feeling of utter helplessness and desolation. Had I come all the way to China for this?

That night in my room, my Father spoke to me. "I have given you today for a few minutes a tiny taste of what thousands of My children continually experience in China. They know what it is to feel cut off, even from their fellow Chinese. When it comes to fellowship, they speak another language, belong to another culture. They are "aliens and strangers" to the world, and likewise the world to them. Some of them are in prison for the sake of My name. Others are in labor camps, hundreds of miles from home, loved ones, and Christian fellowship. I gave you this experience that you might begin to identify with them, pray for them, and encourage others to pray."

A young Christian from mainland China who reached Hong Kong testified to how the hymn "No, Never Alone" had been a tower of strength to her. Reared in a Christian home, she gave her life to Christ at the age of eleven. She went to study at a university thousands of miles from her home town. At the university they used to hold criticism meetings. Because she was a Christian they would put her in the circle and cross-examine her. Then one of the group would read a prepared speech. When they grew tired of this, they would send her away until they wanted to repeat the process. She recalled, "I was very much alone at that time. No one wanted to be seen talking to me. Although living on campus, I ate alone and studied alone."

One evening she was feeling very lonely and heavy laden. As she walked up a nearby mountain the song came to her mind, "No, Never Alone." She started singing the song softly, and then louder, till joy filled her and overwhelmed her. She knew that the Lord was with her.

After graduation she was assigned to a factory job in bitterly cold Manchuria. Again she was a long way from home. They shifted her from factory to factory, giving her the dirtiest and most exhausting work, involving long hours—just because she was a Christian. "My family would never have recognized this dirty factory worker." Many of her colleagues contracted occupational diseases, but God kept her healthy. In the university they had criticized her, but in the factory her treatment was far worse. Here she was condemned as an anti-revolutionary. But again and again she was comforted by the song "No, Never Alone."[108]

The Word of God exhorts us not only to pray for but also to identify with all those who suffer for their Christian faith. "Remember those in prison as if you were their fellow prisoners, and those who are mistreated as if you yourselves were suffering."[109] Surely it has been the power of prayer that has brought such Christians through their ordeals and has even "served to advance the gospel."[110]

A group of itinerant preachers from central China who met for a work conference put out a number of prayer requests, one of which was:

> Please pray for our imprisoned brothers and sisters.
> Lord, give them strength to match their days. Increase
> their inner strength and let it suffer no loss. Manifest
> the power of Your outstretched arm of deliverance, and
> perform a miracle in setting free the imprisoned and
> leading them home. Shorten the terms of those who are
> sentenced to long terms, so that they will have more
> time to do Your work.[111]

As political and economic considerations continue to compel the Chinese Communist party to adopt a "softly, softly" policy towards Christianity (to give the outside world the impression of religious tolerance), its efforts to force the house churches into the Three-Self Movement, and so under control, are also certain to intensify. This is an area of great danger for the future of the church in China. Hence those same itinerant preachers include this further prayer request:

> Ask the Lord to bind heresies and expose the Big
> Harlot's nakedness, so that people will understand and
> escape from her snares. (A note here explains that the
> Big Harlot is the Three-Self movement. The house
> church leaders are comparing the official church to the
> Israelites who committed fornication with the Moabites
> in Numbers 25:1-9).

We need to pray that house church leaders will see the issues very clearly as far as the Three-Self churches are concerned, taking their lead from God and refusing to compromise, rather than being influenced by leaders within the official churches, godly men though some of them may be.

We are commanded to pray for our rulers, "that we may live peaceful and quiet lives in all godliness and holiness."[112] For God to answer such a prayer for China will not necessarily mean the overthrow of the Communist regime, or that it will cease to persecute the church. But it would mean that the country would be saved from a breakdown of law and order such as accompanied the Cultural Revolution, when all Christian activity virtually ceased. As the Scripture goes on to explain, the purpose of such prayer is to facilitate the spread of the gospel. Evangelism came to a halt in the Cultural Revolution, but burst into life when that period ended.

If we feel led to pray for the total destruction of the Bamboo Curtain and for China to join the ranks of the free world, we need to be very sure that this is God's will for this time. If the Communist authorities seem reluctant to open the door any wider than is economically necessary to the "unacceptable face of capitalism" and to so much decadence that goes along with Western culture, who can blame them? Of course we know there are other reasons. How tragic if China were suddenly inundated with Western denominationalism, with every conceivable brand of Christian ministry and organization, teaching and emphasis, all jostling to get on the China church bandwagon. What a good thing that control of the Bamboo Curtain is not left in our hands!

Many with a deep concern for the future of the Chinese church would echo the fear of Tony Lambert of Christian Communications when he says:

> The real danger is that Western Christians, with more zeal than knowledge, will again seek to reimpose denominational structures and cultural attitudes that will undo all that has been accomplished in the providence of God over the last thirty years.

Equally pertinent are the words of the veteran missionary to China, Paul Kauffman:

> We must recognize the cultural maturing of China's church and not permit our culture to again infiltrate and thus deform a church that has, at great price, become truly indigenous.[113]

To help those who may wish to start praying intelligently for the church in China, here is a list of suggested prayer points, including those we have already mentioned:

1. For those in prison or labor camp who are suffering for Jesus' sake. For those who have been arrested and are awaiting trial, and for all under threat of this. For those who are enduring loneliness for Christ's sake.

2. For those at home suffering because loved ones, and perhaps the breadwinner, have been arrested, that they may know God's comfort, protection, and supply.

3. For evangelists and itinerant preachers, who are the "Christian fugitives" of China, and who pay a great price to fulfill their ministry.

4. For leaders, who are under pressure to compromise and lose their liberty in Christ by joining the official church, that they may stand firm, and that the Christians may stand with them.

5. That there may not be animosity between believers of the house churches and those in the Three-Self churches. That believers in the house churches may be able to recognize and receive their brothers and sisters in the Three-Self churches while rejecting the system that they have joined.

6. For the raising up of new leaders—for apostles, prophets, evangelists, shepherds, and teachers, and all those whom God is calling to preach and to witness.

7. That the church as a whole will be nourished and grow strong, knowing its prophetic calling and destiny.

8. That God will overrule the decisions of the Communist authorities so as to grant peace in the land, that the gospel may be fully proclaimed. That God will have the Bamboo Curtain under His control, to facilitate His purpose for His church in China.

9. For the supply of Bibles and Christian literature to meet the growing need, and that Christians taking these into China will act wisely and judiciously.

10. For those whose ministry is preparing and beaming radio broadcasts into China, whether evangelistic, Bible teaching, or leadership-preparation material.

11. For those preparing printed teaching materials and Bible study courses for Christians in mainland China.

12. For Chinese students who have gone to study at Western universities, that Christians may befriend them and lead them to Christ.

13. For the growing number of Christians from the West who are regularly going into China, whether teachers, businessmen, technicians, or students, that the pressures to which they are subjected may not dull their witness for Christ.

14. For the church in Hong Kong, at present ill-prepared for the Communist takeover in 1997, that it may be cleansed and renewed, united and dedicated for the testings that lie ahead.

20

THE WAKING GIANT

Now to him who is able to do
immeasurably more than all we ask or
imagine, according to his power that is
at work within us . . .

Ephesians 3:20

As a land, China is possessed of immense natural resources
and almost unlimited manpower. As a people, the Chinese
have been endowed with fertile minds and outstanding
natural abilities. Isolated for millennia by a sense of their
self-sufficiency and even racial superiority, the people of the
"middle country" are at last relating with the big outside
world. What does the future hold for them?

Two hundred years ago someone asked Napoleon for his
views on China. "China?" replied the Emperor. "There lies a
sleeping giant. Let him sleep, for when he wakes he will
move the world."

On an October morning in 1949, in front of the
"Forbidden City" in the heart of Beijing, Chairman Mao
Zedong gave notice to the world that the "sleeping giant"
had not only wakened, but had gotten to his feet: "The
Chinese people have stood up!"

Across the nation the words were taken up by jubilant
young Communists. "Yes," they cried, "the Chinese people
have stood up at last!"

That was more than thirty-five years ago. It has been an
uphill struggle, and not without some disastrous setbacks,
but China can no longer be viewed as a Third World country
struggling for survival. She has become a member of the
United Nations. She has joined the "nuclear club." She is
even being described as "a candidate superpower." Arnold

Toynbee, that perceptive historian, once said, "The twenty-first century will belong to China." Some with an eye on God's prophetic clock might ask, "Will there be a twenty-first century?" In the world events are taking place with frightening rapidity. The sands of time are running out.

Of far greater significance to us than any political or economic awakening of the Chinese giant is the great spiritual awakening that has been the central theme of this book. Millions are now giving the "thumbs down" to the atheistic philosophy of Marxism, and are turning their faces toward Christ. Just how many of these people are truly regenerated it is difficult to say; but there is no mistaking the trend, and the Communists can do nothing about it. Said Jonathan Chao of the Chinese Church Research Center:

> After ten years of China study and five years of research into the church in China, I have come to the conclusion that in fifteen to twenty years China will become the greatest harvest field in the history of mankind.

That is a thrilling prospect, but it has never been in the heart of Chinese believers to be the nation that is always at the receiving end of God's grace. There has always been the burning desire to reach out to others. China has had much to give. Who can measure the influence of Watchman Nee? As he languished in a Communist prison his teachings reached out to bless the worldwide church. John Sung, the "uncompromising evangelist," is one of many anointed preachers who have blazed a trail for God far beyond the borders of China. Before the Revolution, Chinese Christians, without any prompting from the West, formed their own evangelistic teams and missionary agencies.

The church in China has yet to fully discover her identity in God and to realize her calling and destiny. Is it to be the "greatest harvest *field*," or will it be the "greatest harvest *base*," reaching out to a lost and dying world? Shortly before he died in 1973, Timothy Dzao, "one of China's great pastor evangelists," asked Paul Kauffman to convey this message to the churches of the West:

> I believe that the time has come for the Chinese to preach the gospel in the West. This firstly, because we

should acknowledge our debt to the missionaries who
came to China with the gospel, and secondly, because
God has given us Chinese brilliant minds, and a unique
ability to understand the Scriptures, which were written
in an Oriental context. I believe that God wants us
Chinese to bless the West and lead many to Christ.[114]

A prophetic word? If God plans to use this Oriental
people to bless the West, might He not first use them to bless
other Oriental peoples closer to hand?

When Francis Xavier first brought Christianity to Japan
in 1549 he was impressed to see how successfully the Chinese
had brought Confucianism to that nation. If the Chinese
can do that with Confucianism, he thought, how much more
with the Christian gospel? Believing that China was the key
to the evangelism of Japan, Xavier set sail for China, but he
died on an island off the China coast in 1552. His vision was
never fulfilled.

Though Japan had the gospel first, it was China that was
the scene of the great missionary movement of the last
century. It was China that was destined in this present
century to raise up teachers and preachers to touch the
outside world. And it is now China, despite the oppressive
rule of Marxism, that is now experiencing such a great
turning to Christ. In preparation for what? Perhaps after
500 years Xavier's vision is destined for greater fulfillment
that even he envisaged.

The cross has always loomed large in the thinking and
the experience of the church in China, but never more so
than in the last thirty-five years. Engulfed in a river of
suffering, Chinese Christians have not quailed before the
flood, but, like their master, for the joy set before them have
endured the cross and despised the shame. Is the time soon
to come when God will overthrow every obstacle, satanic
and human, and give His servants a worldwide ministry? Is
that river of suffering to flow out to a waiting world as a river
of blessing?

The last phase of human history prior to Christ's return
in glory is to be a time when, according to His own prophecy,
"This gospel of the kingdom will be preached in the whole
world as a testimony to all nations, and then the end will

come."[115] By the phrase,"*this* gospel of the kingdom," Jesus was pinpointing the sign-and-wonder gospel which He and His disciples had preached as the message that would precede the end of the age.[116] Healings and miracles are to characterize the last phase of gospel preaching, just as they characterized the first. Could we find a church anywhere in the world today so ready for such a worldwide task as is the church in China?

When God finally lifts the Bamboo Curtain, releasing these dedicated emissaries of the cross to join hands with Christians of the free world to gather in the final harvest, will they find us ready and willing to pay the price? Not unless there is a significant change in what Chinese Christians who do reach the West are presently finding. One such was Mrs. Lee, interviewed by Mrs. Marjorie Baker, a former missionary to China. This Chinese lady had been telling of the sufferings that she and her family had endured for thirty years under Communist rule, and then she added:

> I thank God we did not come to Hong Kong in 1948 when we had the opportunity. We might be rich by now in material things, but we would be very poor in spirit. A millionaire could not buy the treasures we now have in Christ.

An old school friend of mine in Hong Kong, constantly in and out of China, told me how many Chinese Christians are disillusioned by the Christianity they find in the West. It is not so much the prosperity as the attitude toward and preoccupation with material things. A former missionary said, "They frequently express a keen disappointment with the shallowness of the church."

In China the believers know they are engaged in spiritual warfare. They know that they are not fighting a government, a system, or an ideology. They are not fighting "flesh and blood," whether Party members, Communist cadres, or government officials. They are not fighting lapsed Christians or those believers who have linked themselves with the Three-Self movement. They are contending against those ruling spirits in the heavenly realms who fight for the kingdom of Satan. But when they reach the West, they find that people do not seem to be aware that there is a war on!

A woman who is a Christian leader in China had been sharing with her visitors from the West something of the sufferings she and her husband and family had had to endure for the sake of Christ. When the visitors expressed their sympathy, she replied:

> Don't feel sorry for us. At least we are constantly reminded that we are in spiritual warfare. We know for whom we are fighting. We know who are our enemies. And we really are fighting. Perhaps we should pray for you Christians outside China. In your leisure, in your affluence, in your freedom, sometimes you no longer realize that you are in a battle.

It is not that the battle in the West is easier than in China. It is just different. In China Satan stalks the land as a roaring lion, seeking whom he may devour. There is no way you can stand as a witness to Christ and avoid meeting him. Either you resist him by faith, and he flees, or you give in to him through fear, and are neutralized. In the West, Satan comes as the beguiling serpent. He entices, he lures, he deceives. It all happens before we are even aware that he has infiltrated our ranks. Slowly, almost imperceptibly, our love grows cool. Preoccupation with things replaces passion for Christ. Witness with our lips becomes the exception rather than the rule. "I'm sure they all know where I stand," becomes our excuse. And because there are so many just like us, no one even whispers the word, "backslider"! East or West—the temptation may be different, but the answer is the same.

Let no one close this book with a sigh, thinking, "It is too high," or "It is too hard." God's will is never beyond our reach; His grace is available to make it accessible. The God who chose us, knowing us better than we know ourselves, is at work within us to make us what He wants us to be. He has also created us for good works which He has prepared in advance for us to do.

Before this age concludes, our Lord Jesus Christ is going to have a glorious and triumphant church that He will be proud to own. His purpose is for you to be part of that final generation of overcomers who—

by the blood of the Lamb, and
by the word of their testimony, and
by not loving their lives, even unto death—

will finally hurl down Satan from the heavens and draw forth the triumphant cry, "Now has come the kingdom of our God."

APPENDIX A

IMPORTANT DATES

1766-1122 B.C.	The Shang Dynasty flourished in the Yellow River valley. This was about the time of Moses.
255-206 B.C.	The Qin (Ch'in) dynasty that gave China its name, produced its first emperor who unified the languages, constructed the Great Wall, and brought much reform.
1644-1911 A.D.	The Qing (Ch'ing or Manchu) dynasty. The Manchus came from the north. Abdication of the last Manchu emperor in 1911 ended 3,600 years of dynastic rule in China.
1807	Robert Morrison, first Protestant missionary to China, arrived in Macao.
1822	First modern-day version of the Bible in Chinese.
1839-1842	The First Opium War, Britain versus China.
1856-1860	The Second Opium War, Britain and France versus China.
1900	Boxer Rebellion. 186 Protestant missionaries martyred.
1912	Sun Yat-sen inaugurated as the first president of the Republic of China. Ousted six weeks later.
1919	Versailles Treaty of World War I that handed Chinese territory to Japan.

1922	Sun Yat-sen restored to power.
1934-1936	The Long March, strategic retreat of the Communist Armies from the Nationalist (Kuomintang) Armies.
1937-1945	The Sino-Japanese War.
1945-1949	Civil War between the Nationalists and the Communists.
1949 (October)	Proclamation in Beijing (Peking) of the People's Republic of China by Mao Zedong (Tse-tung), its first chairman. The Nationalists set up their base in Taiwan.
1951-1952	Land Reform Campaign. Private land confiscated. Campaigns against capitalists.
1952	All missionaries finally driven out of China.
1954	Three-Self Patriotic Movement constituted.
1956	The "Hundred Flowers" Movement.
1958	All Christian denominations finally dissolved.
1958	The Great Leap Forward.
1966-1976	The Great Cultural Revolution.
1971	China admitted to the United Nations.
1976	Deaths of Premier Zhou Enlai (Chou En-lai) and Chairman Mao Zedong. Arrest of the Gang of Four.
1978	Emergence of Deng Xiaoping as No. 1 in China. The Four Modernizations Program aimed at agriculture, industry, defense, and science.

APPENDIX B

CHINA MINISTRIES

For those who wish to be kept up to date with news of what God is doing in China, and of ministries that are reaching the church in that land, the following organizations issue periodical reports, prayer bulletins, magazines, etc:

Asian Outreach, GPO Box 3448, Hong Kong.

Chinese Church Research Center, P.O. Box 312, Shatin Central P.O., N.T., Hong Kong.

China Ministries Department, Christian Communications, P.O. Box 95364, Tsimshatsui, Hong Kong.

Overseas Missionary Fellowship Ltd, China Programme Office, c/o Christchurch, Glebe Road, Bayston Hill, Shrewsbury, SY3 0PZ, U.K.

China Prayer Fellowship, Send Barns Lane, Send, Woking, Surrey GU23 7BS, U.K.

Open Doors, P.O.Box 47, Ermelo, Holland.

Trans World Radio, 45 London Road, Biggleswade, Bedfordshire SG18 8ED, U. K.

Far East Broadcasting Association, 45 High Street, Addlestone, Weybridge, Surrey KT15 1TJ, U. K.

Far East Broadcasting Company, P.O. Box 96789, Tsimshatsui, Hong Kong.

NOTES

Chapter 2

1. The modern Pinyin spelling of Chinese names is used throughout, but where the older Wade-Giles system is more familiar to English readers, this has been put in parentheses.
2. Paul Kauffman, *China: The Emerging Challenge* (Baker Book House, 1982) p. 127. Reprinted by permission, as are subsequent quotations from this book where only author and page number are indicated in the notes.

Chapter 4

3. Kauffman p. 96. 4. Rom. 13:1.

Chapter 6

5. Kauffman pp. 170-71. 6. Mt. 16:18.

Chapter 7

7. Mt. 13:33. 8. Jer. 1:10. 9. Dan. 11:33. 10. Dan. 11:35. 11. Buddhism: with the reopening of Christian churches there has also been a reopening of Buddhist temples, and some resurgence of Buddhism and ancestor worship, but mostly among the older people. 12. Fox Butterfield, *China: Alive in the Bitter Sea* (Times Books, 1982), reprinted by permission.

Chapter 8

13. Mt. 22:21. 14. Rev. 21:2; 17:6. 15. Rev. 18:4.

Chapter 9

16. Kauffman p. 198. 17. Jonathan Chao, Chinese Church Research Center.

Chapter 10

18. "Cadre" is a general term for any worker of the Chinese government or of the Chinese Communist Party. A cadre is roughly equivalent to a civil servant. 19. From *Pray for China,* A Bi-monthly Report (Christian Communications, Hong Kong). 20. Kauffman p. 208. 21. From *Pray for China* (Christian Communications, Hong Kong). 22. *China and the Church Today* (Chinese Church Research Center, Hong Kong). 23. Dan. 4:35 24. Job 33:13 (NASB).

Chapter 11

25. Mt. 5:11-12. 26. Jn. 12:27-28. 27. Acts 5:41. 28. Acts 9:16. 29. Acts 14:22. 30. Phil. 1:29. 31. 2 Cor. 4:7-12. 32. Acts 20:24 (NASB). 33. Carl Lawrence, *The Church in China* (Bethany House Publishers, Minneapolis), reprinted by permission. 34. Jonathan Chao, Chinese Church Research Center.

Chapter 12

35. 1 Thess. 1:6-10. 36. 1 Kings 18:38. 37. *China Prayer Letter,* Dec. 1983 (Chinese Church Research Center). 38. 1 Pet. 5:10. 39. 2 Cor. 4:12. 40. 1 Pet. 1:6,8. 41. 1 Pet. 4:1-2. 42. Rev. 2:10. 43. Acts 4:10. 44. Acts 5:41-42. 45. Watchman Nee, *The Normal Christian Worker.* 46. David Adeney, *China: Christian Students Face the Revolution* (IVP 1973). 47. Dan. 3:18.

Chapter 13

48. David Adeney, *China: Christian Students Face the Revolution* (IVP 1973). 49. 2 Tim. 2:3 (TLB). 50. 1 Cor. 9:24-27 (RSV). 51. Lk. 9:23. 52. 1 Pet. 2:11 (RSV). 53. Watchman Nee, *The Normal Christian Worker.* 54. Jn.4:32. 55. Mt. 26:41. 56. Watchman Nee, *The Normal Christian Worker.* 57. Phil. 4:12. 58. 1 Cor. 4:11. 59. 2 Cor. 12:7-9. 60. 2 Cor. 12:9-10 (italics mine). 61. Heb. 11:37. 62. 2 Cor. 1:9-10. 63. Rev. 2:9. 64. Jas. 2:5. 65. Heb. 10:34. 66. Rom. 12:6-8. 67. Mk. 12:43-44. 68. 2 Cor. 8:2-4. 69. 1 Tim. 6:5,8. 70. Prov. 12:18 (RSV). 71. 1 Pet. 4:19. 72. 1 Pet. 4:15. 73. 1 Pet. 4:16. 74. 1 Pet. 4:12-14. 75. 1 Pet. 2:19,21. 76. 1 Pet. 3:13-16. 77. 1 Pet. 2:23. 78. 2 Cor. 4:17. 79. 2 Cor. 12:10.

Chapter 14

80. Watchman Nee, *Sit, Walk, Stand* (Tyndale House, 1977). 81. Ex. 15:11. 82. Jer. 29:13.

Chapter 15

83. Kauffman p. 229. 84. Carl Lawrence, *The Church in China* (Bethany House Publishers, Minneapolis). 85. Col. 2:20-22. 86. Jn. 18:36. 87. Mt. 6:33. 88. Col. 3:1-2 (RSV). 89. 1 Jn. 2:15. 90. 1 Jn. 2:17. 91. 1 Pet. 2:11. 92. Phil. 3:20. 93. Gal. 6:14.

Chapter 16

94. 1 Cor. 12:9-10. 95. Mk. 16:18. 96. C. E. Cowman, Streams in the Desert (Marshall, Morgan & Scott 1971).

Chapter 17

97. Acts 12:13-15. 98. Kauffman p. 199. 99. Kauffman pp. 194-5. 100. 1 Cor. 14:1. 101. 1 Cor. 14:12. 102. 1 Cor. 14:5.

Chapter 18

103. 1 Cor. 14:26. 104. 1 Cor. 12:7. 105. Heb. 12:25-29. 106. G. H. Lang, *Church Federation*.

Chapter 19

107. Eph. 4:11. 108. From a report in *The Church in China,* Carl Lawrence (Bethany House Publishers, Minneapolis). 109. Heb. 13:3. 110. Phil. 1:12. 111. *China Prayer Letter,* October 1984 (Chinese Church Research Center). 112. 1 Tim. 2:1-2. 113. Kauffman p. 315.

Chapter 20

114. Kauffman p. 158. 115. Mt. 24:14. 116. Mt. 24:23-24; 9:35; 10:7-8.